IMAGES
of America

IOWA CITY

ON THE COVER: This fall 1927 photograph shows a lovely street scene with classic streetlamps and a well-manicured hedge adorning Iowa Avenue between the University of Iowa's Pentacrest and the CRANDIC (Cedar Rapids and Iowa City) viaduct. (Courtesy of the Frederick W. Kent Collection of Photographs, University Archives, the University of Iowa Libraries.)

IMAGES
of America

IOWA CITY

Thomas Schulein

ARCADIA
PUBLISHING

Published by Arcadia Publishing
Charleston, South Carolina

Printed in the United States of America

Library of Congress Control Number: 2024930066

For all general information, please contact Arcadia Publishing:
Telephone 843-853-2070
Fax 843-853-0044
E-mail sales@arcadiapublishing.com

Visit us on the Internet at www.arcadiapublishing.com

For Richard Green, who inspired me to study Iowa City history

A group of students attending a University of Iowa library summer school session is seen in this 1930 photograph. (Courtesy of the Frederick W. Kent Collection of Photographs, University Archives, the University of Iowa Libraries.)

CONTENTS

Acknowledgments   6

Introduction   7

1.   Beginnings and Early History   9

2.   Growth and Neighborhoods   27

3.   Industry, Transportation, and the River   55

4.   The University   77

5.   Worship and Leisure   103

6.   Business and Community   129

ACKNOWLEDGMENTS

When my friend Timothy Walch recommended me as the author of this book, I hesitated at first, thinking it would be a daunting task. Upon further reflection, I realized my intense 10-year record of researching some 40 broad-ranging categories of Iowa City history as well as speaking widely on these subjects had given me a solid base upon which to build.

It has been my pleasure to interview numerous longtime residents. They not only increased my understanding and knowledge but became the inspiration for me to dig a little deeper.

I wish to thank those who helped me in my research and those who provided many of the photographs that I have used. These include Doug Alberhasky, David Arch, Dr. Oscar Beasley, Tom Braverman, Ed Brinton, Ray Bryant, Willis Bywater, Bernie Cremers, Sam Fosse, Dan Gengler, Margaret Hibbs, Phil Hotka, Amy Kanellis, David Keeley, Guenn Kehoe, Virginia Neuzil Kleis, Richard Klinite, Bob Lehman, Michael Lensing, Bud Louis, Joel Myers, John Nash, Brian O'Harra, Doris Preucil, Heather Stockman, Bob White, the staff of Special Collections at the University of Iowa Libraries, and others.

The photographic collection of longtime Iowa City and University of Iowa photographer Fred Kent has provided me with an immense resource of images in the production of this book. Without his images, this work would not have been possible. In addition, the archives of the *Iowa City Press-Citizen* and its predecessors and other historical Iowa City newspapers have proven to be invaluable for information within the captions.

I am also indebted to my editor, Jeff Ruetsche, for his guidance throughout the project and to my wife, Vivian, for reviewing the image captions and her general encouragement.

For convenience, source references are abbreviated as follows:

A	Photograph by the author
SC	Samuel Calvin Collection of Photographs, University Archives, the University of Iowa Libraries
FWK	Frederick W. Kent Collection of Photographs, University Archives, the University of Iowa Libraries

Unreferenced sources are considered to be in the public domain.

INTRODUCTION

The land that would become Iowa City was part of the Louisiana Purchase of 1803 and remained in a succession of six territories of the United States before statehood for Iowa was achieved in 1846. Johnson County was founded in 1837 while part of the Wisconsin Territory. After the formation of the Iowa Territory in 1838, Burlington was chosen as the first territorial capital, but the legislature soon after elected to remove the capital to a place more centrally located. In 1839, Gov. Robert Lucas assigned three men, Chauncey Swan, Robert Ralston, and John Ronalds to select a site in Johnson County to establish a new city to be named Iowa City. Iowa City officially became the territorial capital in 1841.

Swan became the prime mover in the initial work of "building" a new frontier town, which included the supervision of the building of the capitol after the architect left following a dispute. However, before the capitol building could be readied for use, one meeting of the territorial legislature took place in a simple wooden structure known as Butler's Capitol, which was erected entirely with Walter Butler's private funds. Butler was later only partially compensated by the territorial legislature.

Chauncey Swan also operated an early hotel and stagecoach stop and donated land near the central city for a church building, but left early on to join in the California gold rush in 1850 and died at sea upon his return.

Upon the achievement of Iowa statehood in 1846, Iowa City went from territorial capital to state capital. The city was not incorporated until 1853. With continued growth in Iowa, owing the nation's expansion westward, however, the capital was moved in 1857 to Des Moines to be close to the center of the state.

After the arrival of an east–west rail line in 1855, Iowa City, as the western terminus, grew rapidly with a five-fold population increase in the decade of the 1850s. Iowa City is the University of Iowa and the University of Iowa is Iowa City. The two are closely intertwined. Without one, there would not be the other. The university is the city's largest employer and "town and gown" have grown in combination with each other over the university's entire history. However, the university got off to a shaky start after its founding in 1847. Financial concerns plagued early development and the first classes were not held until 1855, and not in a university building at that. Once going, there was no stopping the State University of Iowa, still officially titled that today. Early dynamos such as Gustavus Hinrichs helped establish its reputation early on.

Another rail line reached Iowa City in 1877, locally known as "the Plug," which was an extension of the north–south line of the Burlington, Cedar Rapids, & Northern Railroad. With that, passengers and freight had a means for more direct north–south movement, not afforded by the east–west rail line.

Before the proliferation of the automobile, two more rail lines were established, the CRANDIC interurban, in 1904 and the Iowa City Street Railway, or "streetcar," in 1910.

Pioneers such as Sylvanus Johnson, Peter A. Dey, Robert Finkbine, Samuel Kirkwood, and others brought integrity and everlasting fame to Iowa City. Ardent advocates of civil rights such as the infamous John Brown, and modern-day figures such as Helen Lemme, Elizabeth Tate, Phillip Hubbard, and others have all left their marks. And then there are those who have made contributions to the recording of Iowa City history. Those include such individuals as Clarence Ray Aurner, Gilbert Irish, Jacob Reizenstein, Gerald Mansheim, Lolly Parker Eggers, Irving Weber, Robert Hibbs, Margaret Keyes, Marybeth Slonneger, and others.

Iowa City is noted for many national firsts, as the reader will discover. Numerous individuals have contributed through their sense of community, athletic achievements, scientific endeavors, humanitarian efforts, and work in the arts and entertainment industries. Their stories will be found through a reading of the image captions in this book.

Variously called an "Athens of the West," a UNESCO (United Nations Educational, Scientific and Cultural Organization) City of Literature, and the Greatest Small City for the Arts, Iowa City continues to flourish, attracting new families, University faculty and researchers, business people and retirees, who find world-class medical care and enough sports, arts, and entertainment for all to take in.

The late 1800s saw the startup of much industry, which faded away in the early part of the 20th century, only to find new impetus beginning in the 1950s, industry that is thriving to this day. The establishment of the Procter and Gamble plant in Iowa City came about not without some pushback. Fearing such things as billowing smokestacks and industrial waste, the fears of university and city officials were calmed, after they were taken to Cincinnati, Ohio, and shown just how clean the new plant would be. And, after its establishment, Procter and Gamble worked with the community to focus on establishing a close working relationship. Other clean industrial operations were established in the 1960s and 1970s.

The story of Iowa City is about people, their dreams, and accomplishments, and no history would be complete without telling their stories. It is a tale of much more than historical markers and buildings alone.

In a work of this size, it is impossible to include all of the significant events of the city's 185-year history, and no doubt some things have been overlooked or simply not found inclusion in the limited space allowed. And, in some cases, suitable images could not be obtained for subjects worthy of inclusion.

The Iowa City historical newspaper archives proved invaluable for providing information used in the image captions for this book. Additional information was gleaned from book sources and interviews with many individuals.

It has been my joy to contribute in whatever small way in relating the story of Iowa City. The work of researching history is a labor of love, enriched by the continual uncovering of more and more treasures of the past. It is my sincere hope that the reader will get a broad sense of the rich history that this once-frontier town turned world-class community has to offer.

One

BEGINNINGS AND EARLY HISTORY

This map shows the "first trading post" on the Iowa River south of future Iowa City. It was established around 1826 and administered by Stephen Phelps. Later, John Gilbert arrived and established a trading post. After the two Black Hawk Purchases and the Keokuk Reserve Purchase in 1837, the area could be legally occupied by white settlers for the first time. In July 1838, this land became part of the Iowa Territory, with Burlington as the first territorial capital. The first Johnson County courthouse was in Napoleon. Three commissioners were appointed to meet on May 1, 1939, at Napoleon in order to select an appropriate place in Johnson County to found a new town to be named Iowa City, which would become the new territorial capital. This image is from the 1939 *Palimpsest*.

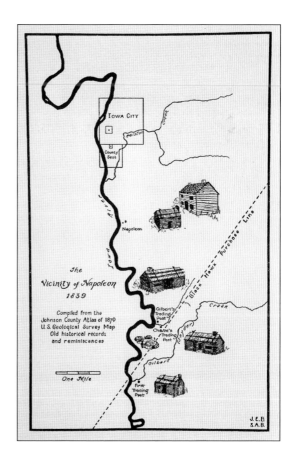

POW · A · SHEEK

A FOX CHIEF.

When Meskwaki chief Poweshiek, along with a large Native American delegation, visited Washington, DC, in 1837, George Cook painted his portrait. Poweshiek dwelled in the area of Napoleon when three men came to Johnson County in 1839 to found Iowa City, and soon after, the chief and his tribe were forced to relocate. Poweshiek's parting message was powerful and has been translated: "Soon I shall go to a new home and you will plant corn where my dead sleep. Our towns, the paths we have made, and the flowers we love will soon be yours. I have moved many times and have seen the white man put his feet in the tracks of the Indian and make the earth into fields and gardens. I know that I must go away and you will be so glad when I am gone that you will soon forget that the meat and the lodge-fire of the Indian have been forever free to the stranger and that at all times he has asked for what he has fought for, the right to be free."

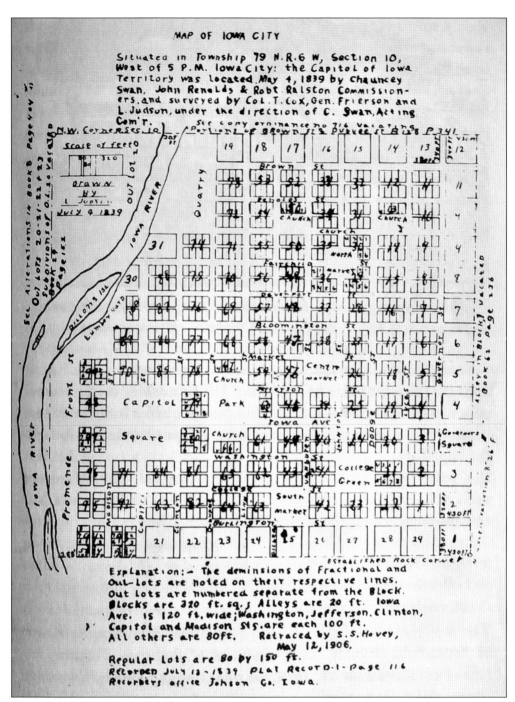

The original plat of Iowa City shows the city laid out in a regular north–south and east–west grid, entirely on the east side of the Iowa River. Each block was numbered, and the legend describes lot dimensions and street and alley widths, with Iowa Avenue to be the widest street at 120 feet. There would be two public sales of lots by auction, with the first in August 1839, followed by another two months later. The money went into the territorial treasury for the construction of the capitol building.

Chauncey Swan was a key figure in early Iowa City history. He was one of three men who selected the site for the new capital city in Johnson County. Swan supervised the building of the capitol, donated land for an early church, and ran a hotel near Capitol Square for many years. After the lure of the gold rush took him to California, he died at sea upon his return. His name has been memorialized by the naming of Hotel Chauncey.

Frederick Macy Irish, who preferred the title of "Captain," was one of the first settlers in Iowa City. He helped haul stone for the building of the capitol. His "Lean Back Hall" served land buyers on the first day lots were auctioned off in Iowa City and could sleep 36 in its one bedroom. Irish's descendants became prominent in local business and state and national affairs.

In 1839, a beautiful site on a bluff overlooking the Iowa River was chosen as the location for the capitol building. Designed by John Rague who left after a dispute, the construction was supervised by Chauncey Swan. After the cornerstone was laid in 1840, the majority of the work was completed by 1842. The east portico seen here came later. Major renovations would take place in the 1920s and 1970s. (FWK.)

Sylvanus Johnson was Iowa City's first brickmaker and supplied bricks in 1840 for the interior walls of the capitol. For the next 20 years, his bricks were used in most of the buildings erected in the city. His business was located on the south side of Burlington Street near today's Northwestern Bell building. During the Civil War, Johnson offered his services to the "graybeard regiment" but his physical condition prevented his serving. His home on Prairie du Chien Road on the north edge of Iowa City still stands.

This stone obelisk marks the original northeast boundary of Iowa City and can be found at the junction of Court and Summit Streets. It shows the mark of wear but endures after almost 200 years. (A.)

A close inspection of the exterior walls of the capitol building reveals the wondrous presence of many fossilized remains, embedded within the ancient limestone. When the spillway of the Coralville Dam was breached during the floods of 1993 and 2008, another reminder of the distant past was created with the unveiling of numerous fossils where the riverbed was washed clean. (A.)

This home at 119 West Park Road was built by Robert Hutchinson in about 1840 outside the original city limits on his 157-acre farm. It is probably the oldest dwelling surviving within the present city limits. With external walls up to 26 inches thick near the foundation, it received a second story in the 1920s and now serves as the University of Iowa Press headquarters. Much of the original Hutchinson property became Manville Heights. (FWK.)

The c. 1851 Bostick House is seen here on North Gilbert Street, moved from its original corner location. It served as Iowa City's first town hall and was a Civil War recruiting station. It now functions as a guesthouse. (A.)

Park House was built in the early 1850s, largely to accommodate early legislators in the period up to 1857, when the capital was moved to Des Moines. In 1861, the building was converted to a girls' boarding school called St. Agatha's Seminary, a nondenominational secondary school, seen in this c. 1890 photograph. In 1909, the building was sold to Albert Burkley, who converted it into a women's dormitory known as Svendi Hall. In 1918, Burkley ran the building as the 27-apartment Burkley Place. Burkley also repurposed an 1855 home he called Ardenia at the south end of Summit Street and ran the Burkley Imperial Hotel on Washington Street, where the Old Capitol Town Center now stands. In the 1980s, structural deficiencies in Park House were identified, resulting in a city order to repair or demolish. Fortunately, this classic structure was saved and following major reconstruction and renovation, it now serves as a 16-unit apartment building.

The Iowa Territorial legislature granted Walter Terrell the first charter for the construction of a mill dam on the Iowa River, which he completed in 1841. Wagons from afar brought grain to be ground by old-fashioned mill stones. Terrell's nearby mansion later became the Red Ball Inn and later yet the Mayflower, a popular meeting spot and restaurant. This c. 1900 photograph is of a view to the north along the river and Dubuque Street, showing advertising for the A.M. Greer jewelry and music businesses on the side of the mill house. (SC.)

The c. 1850 Windrem house built of limestone and brick still stands on the northeast corner of Iowa Avenue and Johnson Street. On this block were stables and sheds constructed by Finkbine and Lovelace in the 1850s for the manufacture of stagecoaches and associated equipment. This house may have served as a stopover for stagecoach passengers. (A.)

Robert Finkbine came to Iowa City from Ohio in the 1850s. He established himself as a master builder, responsible for many university and town structures. He went on to become the superintendent of building for Iowa's five-domed capitol, accounting for every penny spent during its construction. His sons W.O. and E.C. donated land for the first University of Iowa golf course in honor of their father.

Samuel Kirkwood came to Iowa City to enter into business with his wife's brother. He became a lifelong friend of Robert Finkbine, who told Kirkwood, "But you must run" (for the state senate). Kirkwood was launched into a political career that included three terms as Iowa Governor, the US Senate, and Secretary of the Interior under Pres. James A. Garfield. Kirkwood is the namesake for Kirkwood Avenue, Kirkwood Elementary School, and Kirkwood Community College.

Peter Dey was a civil engineer who figured prominently in early eastern canal and railroad construction, and later the construction of the Mississippi and Missouri Railroad that reached Iowa City in 1855. He moved to Iowa City in 1853 and served as an early mayor. When he learned of pending graft in the Credit Mobilier scheme, to his great credit, he "resigned the best position in my profession this country has offered to any man." Dey entered the banking field in Iowa City and became president of the First National Bank, serving until his death in 1911.

The frame 1857 Dey home on North Clinton Street belies its age and now houses the famed Iowa Writers' Workshop program. Dey and his wife, as well as two of their sons and their wives, lived their entire married lives in this home. (FWK.)

The Mechanics' Mutual Aid Association of Iowa City was formed in 1841 to promote the "advancement of the mechanical arts; and whatever may tend to the promotion of education, and the advancement of the arts and sciences." The term mechanic was used to denote a person in the trades such as masonry and carpentry. In 1842, the Iowa Territorial Legislature donated the ground for the building of an academy, specifying that it be devoted exclusively to literary and scientific purposes. The association, consisting of some 40 members, donated their labor and material for the building. The building was completed in 1843 at a cost of three to four thousand dollars, located on the north side of Iowa Avenue near Linn Street. During the first two years, the academy was used as a school with tuition for boys and girls, and in 1848, the medical department of the University of Iowa was located in the building. Over the next 50 years, the building was used as the university's first classrooms, a dormitory, a teaching hospital for the university's medical college, the founding of Mercy Hospital, and other purposes. In 1855, when the first classes were held for the university, there were less than 50 students and a university library of only about 150 volumes in a room only about four feet square. In 1897, the academy building was demolished to make way for a new university hospital. The cornerstone of the Mechanics' Academy has been preserved and is located within a wall inside the east entrance of the University of Iowa Medical Laboratory. (SC.)

This is a daguerreotype by early photographer Isaac Wetherby, showing the first annual Johnson County Agricultural and Mechanical Society Fair taking place on the capitol grounds in October 1853. An ox-drawn wagon is seen conveying melons. A crowd of up to 5,000 turned out for the event. No admission was charged and expenses were $372 and receipts $380, leaving a balance of $8 to apply to the next year's fair, held in September. (FWK.)

This 1854 Isaac Wetherby daguerreotype shows the east side of Clinton Street opposite the Pentacrest. Merchants' names are prominent on the storefronts, which include an early land office. It is believed that the building at the upper right that appears tallest may still exist, recently serving as a more than half-century home for the McDonald Optical Company. (FWK.)

Beginning in the 1860s, the creation of "bird's-eye view" maps for cities and villages was common. The process involved an artist, who would walk the streets of a town while sketching its buildings, streets, and other landmarks. Often, as in this 1868 view of Iowa City, sites would be numbered and keyed to a list printed at the bottom of the view. Details were important, but the maps were not generally drawn to scale. After completion, views were printed and sold to local residents who took pride in their communities. A steamboat is depicted on the Iowa River on this map. Although a small number of steamboats did reach Iowa City from the Mississippi River, the last one to do so was about two years before this image was produced. (Library of Congress.)

Walter Butler hastily erected this wooden structure near today's downtown Panchero's building, to house an early session of the state legislature before the Old Capitol was ready for occupancy. Butler used his own funds, for which he was later only partially compensated. The building, seen here after it was moved in 1856, was demolished in 1892.

This 1923 photograph is a view from Folsom Heights, where the College of Nursing now stands, looking to the southeast. Gilman Folsom came to Iowa City in 1841, built the home seen here in about 1851, and operated a ferry on the Iowa River, near today's Iowa Avenue Bridge. Folsom was an attorney and state legislator. At far left is 1912 MacLean Hall on the Pentacrest, and the Old Armory is seen at the bottom left. Some early Iowa City Chautauquas were held on Folsom Heights. (FWK.)

Finkbine & Lovelace,
MASTER BUILDERS,
Architects and Superintendents,

ALSO MANNFACTURERS OF AND DEALERS IN

Sash, Doors, Blinds, Window Frames, Mouldings, and all kinds of

DRESSED LUMBER,

Hand Rails, Newel Posts, Banisters, Scroll Sawing and

TURNING DONE TO ORDER.

Shop Corner Burlington and Gilbert Sts. Factory W. S. Gilbert bet. Court and Harrison Sts., Iowa City, Iowa.

Plans and specifications furnished on short notice.

This advertisement appeared in the 1868 Iowa City Directory. Robert Spencer Finkbine and Chauncy F. Lovelace established a reputation as master architects and builders as Finkbine & Lovelace and were responsible for many homes, businesses, and university buildings in Iowa City. North Hall on the Pentacrest and the College Block on College Street are two examples. They also built manufacturing buildings and stables used in conjunction with stagecoach construction in Iowa City and contracted for work on the Iowa School for the Blind in Vinton, Iowa.

The c. 1854 Nicking House on Market Street was constructed by the firm of Finkbine & Lovelace and is one of few Iowa City structures surviving built of sandstone. (A.)

The Sanxay-Gilmore house at 109 East Market Street faces an uncertain future. The building is probably from the 1850s. Although doubtful, some consider it the oldest surviving residence in Iowa City. Originally in the Sanxay family, the home was purchased by University of Iowa president Eugene Gilmore in 1946. In 2018, it was sold by Gloria Dei Lutheran Church to the university. (A.)

At the end of 1841, two-year-old Iowa City with a population of about 1,000 was more than well-served by three newspapers, which all began that year. All were weeklies. *The Iowa City Standard*, seen here, was aligned with the Whig Party, and the *Iowa City Argus* and *Iowa Capitol Reporter* were organs of the Democratic Party. (A.)

This tiny native yellow-brown sandstone home on North Johnson Street survives as one of the oldest structures in Iowa City. With external walls about 16 inches thick, it dates to as early as the 1840s. (A.)

After Robert Lucas, former governor of Ohio, became the first governor of the Iowa Territory in 1838, he had this home constructed in 1844, south of Iowa City on the grounds of what has become known as Plum Grove. Seen here before its restoration, it is now open for seasonal tours. (FWK.)

Two

GROWTH AND NEIGHBORHOODS

The Johnson County Savings Bank at the left margin of this photograph identifies the image as 1872 or later. The view is of the south side of Washington Street, adjacent to Capitol Square, later known as the Pentacrest. In addition to the many thriving businesses, a popular hotel, the Burkley, was at the right end of the block beyond the edge of the photograph. In 1911, the three-story savings bank was demolished and replaced with a six-story structure, today serving as MidWestOne Bank. (Daguerreotype by Isaac Wetherby, FWK.)

Dr. Jesse Bowen was an Iowa City physician who was an ardent abolitionist. In February 1859, he harbored John Brown at his home at 914 Iowa Avenue, no longer extant.

Fiery abolitionist John Brown came through Iowa City in February 1859 with a group of slaves brought from Missouri to convey them by rail to Chicago and beyond to their eventual freedom in Canada. Brown led a failed attack on the federal arsenal in Harpers Ferry, Virginia, later in the year, in October. Brown was sentenced and hanged, becoming for some a martyr and symbol of emancipation.

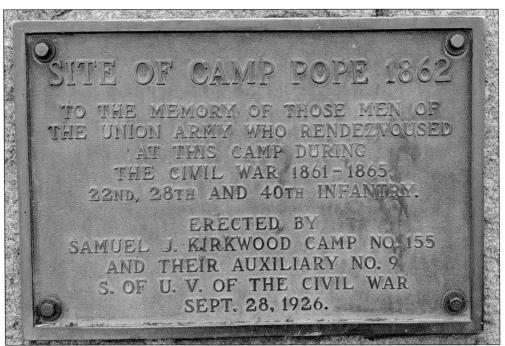

SITE OF CAMP POPE 1862
TO THE MEMORY OF THOSE MEN OF
THE UNION ARMY WHO RENDEZVOUSED
AT THIS CAMP DURING
THE CIVIL WAR 1861-1865,
22ND, 28TH AND 40TH INFANTRY.

ERECTED BY
SAMUEL J. KIRKWOOD CAMP NO. 155
AND THEIR AUXILIARY NO. 9
S. OF U. V. OF THE CIVIL WAR
SEPT. 28, 1926.

This plaque is found on the Longfellow Elementary School grounds, the location of the 1862 Civil War Camp Pope. Great crowds gathered during assemblages of the soldiers, who boarded trains at the nearby Johnson Street depot, on their way to war. Many of these young men would never return. Another camp in Iowa City was Camp Fremont, located in an area north of the present Iowa City Airport. Iowa City contributed many soldiers to the war effort and the State of Iowa sent the largest percentage of eligible men of any state in the Union. (A.)

Johnny Hendricks, aged 11 or 12 when he died, was a drummer boy in the Civil War. His tombstone, located in the original part of Oakland Cemetery, is a grim reminder of the tragedy of the conflict. Land for the cemetery was donated by the territorial legislature to the city in the 1840s. (A.)

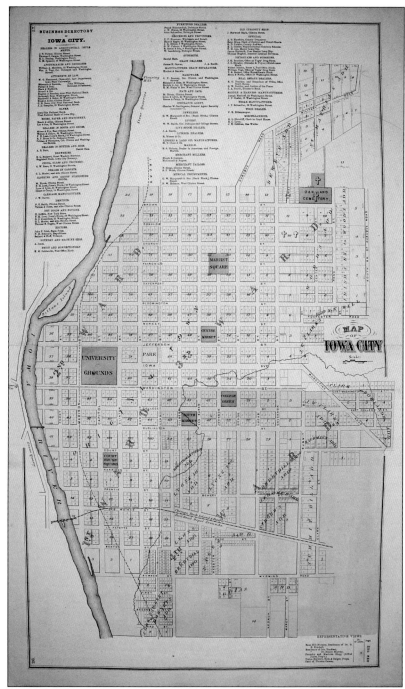

Although there were dwellings on the west side of the Iowa River by 1870, the city limits were still confined to the east side of the river. This 1870 map reveals that Iowa City has more than doubled in area since its founding, with many new additions appearing, mostly to the south. The city has been divided into four wards. The four-block square University Grounds is the extent of the university, and Dillon's Island shown in the Iowa River would be lost in the late 1800s. A business directory is provided at the top of the map. (Map Collection, University of Iowa Libraries.)

This c. 1906 photograph shows the c. 1858 Court Street home of Nicholas Oakes, an early Iowa City brickmaker, whose annual output was about 800,000 bricks, made from clay taken from just north of Longfellow School. Later, Grant Wood purchased the home and lived there from 1936 until his untimely death in 1942. Now owned by attorney Jim Hayes, the home has been beautifully restored. Adjacent buildings to the north along Burlington Street are part of the University of Iowa Grant Wood Art Colony.

This 1890s image of the Pentacrest offers a view to the northwest. The grounds are edged with fencing and wooden plank sidewalks and Washington Street at left is unpaved. From the left are the Medical Building, South Hall, Old Capitol, and North Hall. In 1901, a fire in the Medical Building destroyed it and nearby South Hall. The trees are probably young elms that would later dominate the landscape. (FWK.)

31

In this c. 1895 winter scene, the 1876 Centennial Iowa Avenue Bridge is seen at right. Behind it, the grandstand for the university's baseball diamond can be seen. The advertising sign near the center foreground announces, "Denecke and Yetter, the Big Store, Dry Goods and Cloaks," a downtown Iowa City merchant. All of the homes in this view would be removed by the 1920s. Along the crest of the ridge near the background are seen from left, Old Dental, North Hall, Old

Capitol, South Hall, the Medical Building, and downtown businesses. In front of Old Capitol are the Armory and Power Plant, the water closet, and a livery. At left, just behind Old Dental and North Hall is Science Hall, which would be moved in 1905. In the skyline at left are the steeples of St. Mary's Church and the Congregational church. (SC.)

This mid-1890s photograph is a view looking north on Dubuque Street at the intersection with College Street. A horse-drawn "sprinkle wagon," for dust control on the unpaved streets, appears in the left foreground while a wagon is moving opposite. The 1850s Koza building is at the corner in the right foreground. Also at right, the "HAR" represents Kane's Harness and Buggy store. Note the simplistic street light appearing at the top of the image. The conical dome of Close Hall is seen in the left background. (Special Collections, University of Iowa Libraries.)

This 1913 image shows today's Johnson County Court House, begun in 1899. Four county courthouses preceded it, including a frame one in the pre-Iowa City settlement of Napoleon. (Photograph by John W. Carville, FWK.)

In 1899, Willard F. Main platted the rural subdivision of East Iowa City. He built a large jewelry manufactory at its north end. In spite of a vigorous newspaper advertising campaign, his lots sold slowly, and it was not until the 1950s that the largest growth was seen. Main envisioned the street railway depicted on the plat, but it was never developed. (Map Collection, University of Iowa Libraries.)

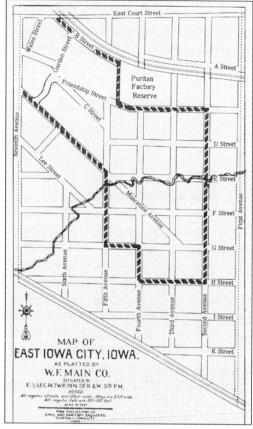

The house seen in this photograph was built in the 1850s for John Powell on the northeast corner of Linn and College Streets. The property extended 150 feet north to the alley and east to the Trinity Episcopal Church, making it one of the largest residential lots in the city. The house was razed in the 1920s, later replaced by a DX service station and today is the site of the Meardon, Sueppel and Downer law firm. (FWK.)

This 1910 photograph shows the 1904 Iowa City Public Library, built with the help of Carnegie funds. Along with a 1963 addition, it served the city until 1981, when a new library was constructed on the west side of Linn Street. The three or four homes in the image are illustrative of how early Iowa City dwellings were part of the downtown area. (SC.)

Four new elementary schools were built in 1917–1918 to replace the antiquated 1850s ward schools. Longfellow Elementary, shown here, and Sabin and Mann were of a similar architectural style, whereas the Kellogg School on the site of today's VA hospital was much smaller and of a different design. (A.)

The Iowa City Post Office was built in 1904, seen here in 1915. In 1930, while undergoing expansion, the C.O.D. Laundry on Iowa Avenue served as temporary post office quarters. In the late 1970s, the post office was moved to South Clinton Street. (FWK.)

Opened in 1981, the Iowa City Senior Center is an award-winning facility that offers classes, lectures, participation in musical organizations, dance instruction, and many other activities. (Bob Lehman.)

Veterans Day was celebrated as Armistice Day, when initiated on November 11, 1918, the date of this parade moving south on Clinton Street in front of the Pentacrest. A long line of cadets/soldiers is visible for several blocks. In 1954, Congress replaced Armistice Day with Veterans Day. A magnificent row of elm trees runs along the west side of Clinton Street. (FWK.)

This view shows the university's Hubbard Park in about 1915. The block suffered a number of floods in the 1800s and early 1900s, so property values were low. The corner building is the Rinella grocery. The university acquired the land and by the mid-1920s, all of the houses were removed and the area was developed into an athletic field. The Rinella family moved their business to Clinton Street across from the Pentacrest, and the business later became the Airliner. (FWK.)

This 1970s image is of Central Junior High School, built as the Iowa City High School in 1903. The building was sold to Mercy Hospital in 1983 to make way for a Medical Center Plaza and parking facility. (Oscar Beasley.)

When the building site for a new high school was chosen in 1938, it was argued that it was too far out of town. It did not take long for city growth to overtake the school and expand far beyond to the east. (Margaret Hibbs.)

Tuberculosis was a significant disease in the United States in the early 20th century, with up to one in four TB victims dying. After the Iowa State Legislature appropriated funds to build a sanatorium, a site was chosen about six miles northwest of Iowa City along the interurban railroad line. Established in 1908, the site was named Oakdale for the large stand of giant oaks. Oakdale grew to consist of many buildings, including hospital units, a poultry house, and one or more barns to house about 50 Holstein cows. Housing units were also built for doctors, nurses, and staff. Farming came to an end at Oakdale in 1964. By 1966, the sanatorium was the only institution in Iowa treating TB patients, but in 1981, TB treatment came to an end there, with the last patient transferred to the University of Iowa Hospitals and Clinics. Many viewed Oakdale not as a hospital, but as a community, complete with its own monthly magazine, post office, fire department, dairy farm, slaughterhouse, and pasteurizing plant. In this undated photograph, three women are seen sharing a comfortable room. The casters observed on each bed allowed for ease of transfer to the outside onto open-air porches. (Oakdale Sanatorium Records, Special Collections and Archives, the University of Iowa Libraries.)

Iowa City was experiencing growing pains at the beginning of the 20th century, with many new subdivisions sprouting up. The interurban (CRANDIC) line, established in 1904, also had an impact. In the Manville area alone were Blacks Second Addition (1908), the Chautauqua Heights Addition (1908), the Suburban Heights Addition (1909), the Manville Addition (1909), and the Manville Heights Addition (1910). East Iowa City was founded in 1899, the Varsity Heights Addition in 1903, and the Rundell Addition in 1908, along with a streetcar system in 1910. In 1910, a measure was put before the voters of Iowa City and Johnson County, asking if the city limits should be expanded to the larger outline shown. Not surprisingly, many voters outside the city limits feared increased taxes and saw no need for annexation. Nonetheless, the measure passed, and by this one act, all of these recent additions, as well as much undeveloped land were taken into Iowa City, effectively doubling its size.

The University Hospital was built in stages, beginning in 1898. This 1907 view is looking north on Linn Street, across Iowa Avenue. St. Mary's Church at left was concerned that a disruption in Linn Street would hamper access to the church from the south, so a sidewalk was provided, as seen to the left of the hospital. A survey of the medical school in 1910 resulted in a declaration of serious deficiencies and so much as recommended closure, but the university made changes that kept the hospital viable. Today's University Hospital is a world-class institution. (FWK.)

This 1930 aerial view is looking west, showing the new University Hospital on the west side of the Iowa River at center and the earlier children's hospital at right. The recently built football stadium is at upper left with University Heights beyond that. The original 18-hole university golf course lies west of University Hospital. (FWK.)

This home is representative of the large 1900-era homes that dominated a three-block stretch of South Summit Street. Many had iron fencing and most had large setbacks, carriage houses, and spoke of grandeur. Most of these homes remain in good repair. Summit Street was so named because of its high elevation. (A.)

Dr. F.C. Titzell built Iowa City's first apartment building on South Summit Street in 1916. It was controversial and received some pushback from owners of the stately mansions in the area. Each apartment was outfitted with a Murphy bed, an oak buffet, a claw-footed bathtub, a speaking tube, and a connection to a central vacuum system. Since 1947, residents have owned their own units, and the building was placed in the National Register of Historic Places in 1996. This photograph was taken in the 1930s. (FWK.)

University Heights was established by Lee and George Koser as a new subdivision of Iowa City. They offered liberal terms to buyers and sold their first lots on Labor Day in 1924. Shamefully, they offered their lots "for the sole use and benefit of the Caucasian Race." Competition for the sale of lots in Iowa City was keen. The Morningside Addition on Iowa City's east side was also established in 1924, offering 130 lots. The *Iowa City Press-Citizen* stated that over 1,000 lots were available to buildings during the 1924-25 time period. This 1929 photograph captured University Heights, still in its infancy. Objection to school taxation led to autonomy through incorporation in 1935. Expansion to the west took place, but by the early 1970s, University Heights was completely surrounded by Iowa City, becoming perhaps the only city in America that is completely surrounded by only one other city. Over the years, there have been overtures for annexation into Iowa City, but each was turned down by the voters of University Heights. In recent years, the development of a commercial property along Melrose Avenue as well as a new hotel have helped to bolster University Height's tax base. University Heights has a somewhat controversial reputation as a speed trap along Melrose Avenue. (FWK.)

As if out of fairyland, this quaint, mysterious-looking cottage was built by Howard F. Moffitt, a man without formal training in the construction business. Moffitt built over 100 houses in Iowa City in the decades of the 1920s, 1930s, and 1940s, often using very unconventional materials: items from dumpsites, chair backs, sawdust for insulation, and even wooden toilet seats for plaster lath. Homes were often built with stone exteriors. Many homeowners have declared that there is not a square corner to be found in any room. When her father waited for his daughter to approach this home on one Halloween night, she told him she was scared "because a real witch lived there!" (A.)

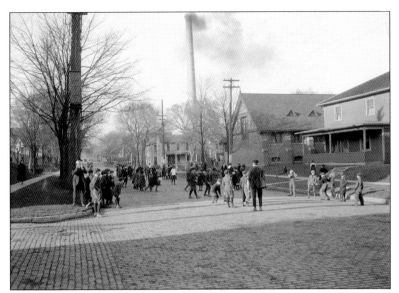

Children are seen at play on Gilbert Street in this c. 1921 image. The 1908 Unitarian church is seen at center right. Apparent are the brick streets that were predominant in the day and the smokestack that served a university laundry building near the corner of Iowa Avenue and Gilbert Street. (FWK.)

This 1939 photograph shows the 200 block of East College Street looking west. The Plaza Café and Brenneman Seeds, at right, occupied space vacated by the *Iowa City Press-Citizen* two years earlier, when it moved to its new building on East Washington Street. The light-colored corner building at center was demolished to make way for a new Penny's store and all of the buildings in the block in the foreground, as well as the other corner's three-story building with mansard roof, would succumb to urban renewal in the 1970s. (FWK.)

This 1940 photograph looking east on Washington Street was taken near the south edge of the Pentacrest. The rails are part of the CRANDIC (interurban) railroad that ran between Iowa City and Cedar Rapids from 1904 to 1953. The Kampus Hotel is seen at right in a block that also had the Burkley Imperial Hotel. The Iowa State Bank building is the six-story structure in the next block and further down is Hotel Jefferson. In the background at left, the clock tower of city hall can be seen. (FWK.)

The new field of gerontology was organized in the 1940s. In the first 50 years of the 20th century, the US population doubled, with the over 65 age group quadrupling and in 1953, Iowa ranked third nationally in the percentage of citizens over 65. This photograph was made at the fourth annual gerontology conference, held at the University of Iowa in 1955. The university also created an Institute of Gerontology. (FWK.)

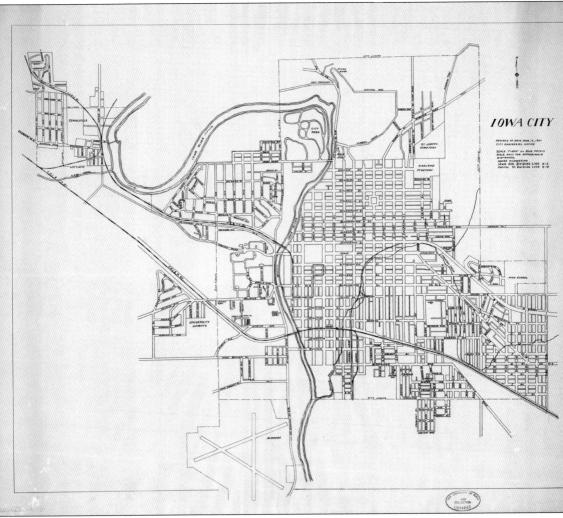

This 1947 Iowa City map shows University Heights at mid-left and a very small Coralville, which had less than 1,000 residents, at upper left. The Morningside Addition at middle right represents the northeast limit of the city. Iowa City was on the eve of a building boom that began in the 1950s. (Map Collection, University of Iowa Libraries.)

This 1940s photograph, looking west along Washington Street, shows several businesses directly south of the Pentacrest. Included are the Singer Sewing Center, a Maid-Rite restaurant, a garage (possibly the Beck Motor Co.), and the Burkley Hotel, the oldest hotel in Iowa City. Built in the 1860s, the Burkley building, along with all of the rest of these businesses would be razed during the 1970s urban renewal program. (FWK.)

This c. 1948 aerial photograph of the Pentacrest shows a multitude of elm trees, most of which were lost to Dutch elm disease a decade or so later. Today's one remaining elm is the certified largest elm in Iowa. The symmetrical array of five buildings is seen as well as North Hall and Old Dental on the far right, north of Old Capitol. At upper left are trailers that were brought in to house married veteran students to help with a severe postwar housing shortage. Since 1840, there have existed at least 19 buildings in the area of the Pentacrest. (FWK.)

Post-World War II, a housing shortage became a serious problem at the University of Iowa, especially when married veterans inquired for quarters. Units were constructed with Federal Public Housing Authority supervision, and as such, only veterans were eligible for the housing. This aerial photograph taken in 1948 shows the largest temporary housing area on campus, comprised of barracks established on the east side of the original Finkbine Field golf course. Known as Finkbine Park, it contained 143 barracks, housing 286 families. The golf course can be seen at the top of the image. Today, this area is occupied by the College of Dentistry. (FWK.)

This young family shown by the Old Capitol c. 1948 probably lived in temporary housing provided for married veterans and their families. Families as large as nine were known to live in one of the small barracks units on campus. The last of the temporary units were removed in 1975. (FWK.)

The federal government also provided these trailers that were established on the east side of the Iowa River between Burlington Street and Iowa Avenue. Subsequently, more trailers, barracks units, and some Quonsets were erected, utilizing just about every green space on campus. Even an area abutting Kinnick Stadium was used for barracks housing. (FWK.)

Henry Black went all out after officials in Iowa City asked him to provide housing for students during the shortage. At odds with the city over building codes, he constructed an array of housing units often using bizarre ornamentation such as bowling balls and tombstones. His amusing newspaper ads declared such things as, "There is not now, never was and never will be another place like Black's Gaslight Village." The village later became somewhat Bohemian in nature, attracting students in the Iowa writing programs and others. A salesman for G.C. Merriam and Company with an MA degree, Black was truly one of a kind. (A.)

Seeds of urban renewal were planted in Iowa City in 1959, with the formation of the Citizens Advisory Committee. With federal help, the controversial program of demolition in the downtown area began in the early 1970s. The buildings seen here on College Street were all removed and replaced by the Old Capitol Mall. The Annex, at right, was a popular bar that was reestablished on First Avenue and now does business as Shakespeare's. (Dr. Oscar Beasley.)

This photograph was taken during the urban renewal process, looking north on Dubuque Street from Court Street, past where the street was later interrupted by the Holiday Inn. Many homes existed in or just outside of the renewal area and were either razed or moved. The corner seen here is now occupied by a parking ramp and the Iowa City Transportation Center. (Dr. Oscar Beasley.)

Urban renewal claimed all of the buildings in the left foreground with the exception of Hotel Jefferson and the two adjoining light-colored buildings next to the hotel. The demolished buildings were replaced by Plaza Centre One. (Dr. Oscar Beasley.)

This c. 1980 photograph shows the new Old Capitol Mall (now Old Capitol Town Center) built south of the Pentacrest, just after its completion. At the far end is a parking ramp and, beyond that, a bank building. (Bob Lehman.)

With the critical post–World War II housing shortage, some thought the answer was prefabricated housing. A brilliant engineer named Carl Strandlund convinced the federal government that he could build enameled steel homes in great numbers to help satisfy the need. However, between 1947 and 1950, only about 2,700 of these homes were built. Strandlund's noble experiment failed and after securing over $30 million in loans from the federal government, foreclosure proceedings against his Lustron Corporation were ordered. The enameled steel home pictured here is in East Iowa City, displaying its original exterior steel panels and steel roof tiles. This is one of seven examples of Lustron homes in the Iowa City area. (A.)

The 3,000 parts for each home were delivered on a single semi-tractor-trailer and utilized local builders to erect the home on a concrete slab. The characteristic zigzag/downspout trellis combination was featured on the front corner of each home. Realtor Roland Smith was the Iowa City dealer for Lustron. (Lustron Corporation.)

Three

INDUSTRY, TRANSPORTATION, AND THE RIVER

A fly-in event hosted at the Iowa City airport is seen in this 1929 photograph. In this same year, the airfield at Iowa City became a municipal airport when the city acquired the 191-acre parcel of land comprising the airport site. (FWK.)

The original Mississippi & Missouri Railroad depot from the 1850s is shown in this photograph. In the spring of 1856, a large group of Mormon immigrants arrived here. Unlike the Mormon group, which arrived in 1847 and moved on to Deseret (future Utah) in wagons, this later group constructed handcarts with which to make the journey.

A crowd is seen waiting for an excursion train at the 1898 Wright Street Rock Island Depot in this c. 1913 photograph. The cylindrical tower seen in the middle background is the water reservoir for the steam engines of the day, and a streetcar can be seen behind the tower. (FWK.)

This tunnel under today's Iowa Interstate Railroad tracks has been described as a Civil War–era structure, without a verified build date. Often used by children at play, it carries the local name of Dead Man's Cave. It was used for personal passage under the rail tracks before a safer modern tunnel was built for bicycles and foot traffic in 2001. (A.)

The passenger and freight depots for the 1877 Burlington, Cedar Rapids, & Northern Railroad (BCR&N) were on the location of today's Robert A. Lee Recreation Center parking lot. The rail line served as a link to the main north-south BCR&N line east of Iowa City and until the CRANDIC opened in 1904, was the only means of rail travel to Cedar Rapids. The rail line into Iowa City probably had little economic importance, and by 1930, most of the track between the main line east of Iowa City and this depot had been removed.

The Iowa City Flint Glass Manufacturing Company produced an inferior grade of glass goblets, plates, and other glassware for only about 20 months before going bankrupt in 1883. Although imitations have surfaced, the originals have become collector's items. Other early industry included the Close Linseed Oil manufactory and the Iowa City Packing and Provision Company, both of which were gone by the 1890s. (A.)

The Rate Glove Company plant is seen in this c. 1908 photograph, after moving into the defunct Iowa City Flint Glass Company building. Rate had the misfortune of burning four times at various locations. The company began making husking gloves but later made about 250 patterns of gloves and mittens. Other one-time Iowa City glove companies included Iowa Glove, Hawthorne Glove, and the Ira Curtis Glove Factory. (FWK.)

Early attempts at improving Iowa City's streets included the application of macadam, a form of crushed rock. Macadamized roads were dusty and during heavy rains, could wash out and so, with the decision to use paving bricks, work began in 1895 on College Street. In this 1895 photograph, a section of Clinton Street along the Pentacrest is being prepared to receive bricks. First, a sand and gravel base was applied and compacted with the steam roller seen at right. Most of the limestone curb has been set into place. The work-intensive labor of applying the bricks was the final step, along with brushing dry sand into the interstices. Today, some 26 blocks of the original brick streets remain, mainly in the original city. The wavy, irregular surfaces serve a kind of traffic-calming function. (Photograph by Laurence Welsh, courtesy of Margaret Hibbs.)

The O.S. Kelly Company of Ohio established a plant on Sheridan Street in 1899, manufacturing small gasoline engines and farm machinery. In the same year, the Boerner-Fry manufacturing facility was built on the corner of Gilbert and Washington Streets to manufacture vanilla extracts and other products. Both companies were short-lived and gone by the early 1900s.

PURITAN MANUFACTURING CO.

Makers of { *High Class Jewelry and Novelties in Rolled Gold Plate and Solid Gold Front*

Largest Factory of its Kind in the United States
IOWA CITY, IOWA

¶ *We refer the few merchants in the United States who are not trading with us to the thousands of satisfied merchants who are.* ¶ *Over 600 satisfied regular customers in Iowa alone.*

OUR GOODS ARE SOLD ON THE MONEY BACK IF NOT SATISFIED PLAN

You Are Invited to Inspect Our Factory

Willard Main built his jewelry factory in East Iowa City in 1900 but, not long after, sold it and pursued other business interests. Main and his successors billed the factory as the largest of its kind in the United States, turning out a wide variety of merchandise. (Special Collections, the University of Iowa Libraries.)

This c. 1900 photograph shows unidentified persons in the yard of Willard Main's home in his new subdivision of East Iowa City. After moving to Cedar Rapids, the home was passed between new owners, became the Putnam Nursing Home for a time, and is now a private residence, near the west end of Friendship Street. (Brian O'Harra.)

In this c. 1930 image, an Englert Ice Company truck is seen getting ready to load. The Englert Ice Company cut ice from the Iowa River for almost 50 years, once proclaiming it to be thick, clear, crystal, natural ice "from the running water of the Iowa River." Irving Weber wrote that "9,000 tons of ice were harvested the Christmas vacation of 1917," but was lost during the June 1918 flood. In the era before electric refrigerators, ice delivery to homes was vital. (FWK.)

The Iowa River did not always freeze well enough to support ice skating. However, in this c. 1920 scene, a large group of skaters is seen, with two men holding hockey sticks. People sometimes fell through the ice, with one young boy losing his life after falling through thin ice where the Englert Ice Company cut ice along the river. (FWK.)

In this 1920s photograph, a crowd is seen on the bank of the Iowa River as a number of canoes are cast off. Noticeably absent are life vests. (FWK.)

SHIP A CANOE
... TO ...
MID RIVER
∴ OR SOME OTHER POINT ON THE ∴
Interurban Railway
... AND FLOAT DOWN ...
THE IOWA RIVER

∴ FOR PARTICULARS, INQUIRE OF ∴

F. D. LINDSLEY, AGENT
IOWA CITY

ISAAC B. SMITH, GEN. TRAFFIC MGR.,
CEDAR RAPIDS
379

This 1909 advertisement offers the services of the CRANDIC to ship canoes to various locations upstream for a float trip back to Iowa City. (Special Collections, University of Iowa Libraries.)

At 120 feet wide, Iowa Avenue was the widest street in the original city. It could have just as aptly been named Iowa Boulevard. This c. 1915 image shows the presence of numerous hitching posts at left. A reminder that horsepower would soon be a thing of the past is the lone car parked along the street in the background. (FWK.)

Awnings on storefronts feature prominently in this c. 1915 view looking south along Clinton Street, across from the Pentacrest. The new Johnson County Savings Bank building (now MidWestOne) is the tallest structure. This was a transition period in which horses and carriages mixed with automobiles, with "road apples" evident on the roadway. (FWK.)

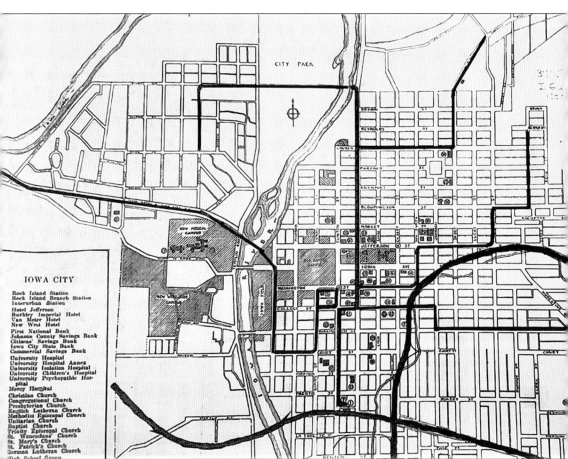

On this 1920 map, four separate passenger rail systems are shown. Included are the transcontinental line of the Chicago, Rock Island & Pacific across the bottom of the map, the curved BCR&N line coming in from the right (east), the CRANDIC interurban line coming in from the west (left), and the Iowa City streetcar with its many branches. The Chicago and Rock Island Railroad ended passenger service in 1970. Today, the line is owned by the Iowa Interstate Railroad, conveying only freight. The BCR&N line was an arm of the North-South Burlington, Cedar Rapids & Northern line, eventually giving over to the Chicago & Rock Island and ending service to and from the east by the early 1930s. The CRANDIC, an interurban line, connected Iowa City and Cedar Rapids and, for a time, Lisbon and offered passenger and some freight service from 1904 until 1953. The 27 miles of track between Iowa City and Cedar Rapids had as many as 60 stops, with the electric cars running as fast as 80 miles per hour. Streetcar service came late to Iowa City, beginning in 1910, and coursed along five routes. After only about 20 years, it gave way to the vastly superior bus route system. (Map Collection, University of Iowa Libraries, markings by author.)

This c. 1910s photograph shows a truck stuck in the mud on unpaved Jefferson Street. The university's law building, now Gilmore Hall, appears in the background. (FWK.)

This 1910s photograph of a MECCA (mechanical, electrical, civil, chemical, and architectural [engineering]) parade float states the need for road improvement, something that was already underway on downtown streets. MECCA week was an annual engineering students' jubilee that included a parade and other events. Behind the float, "Iowa Union," which was in the former Universalist Church building, can be seen. Soon after this photograph was made, the Iowa Union moved across the street to the south in the old St. James Hotel building, which burned in 1916 and was replaced with today's Dey Building, housing Iowa Book. (FWK.)

This c. 1935 photograph shows a view to the south from the Pentacrest. The university's engineering building is prominent on the right. A variety of automobiles of the day are seen as well as a small pickup truck at right. (FWK.)

This 1940 photograph shows the Nall Motors showroom on East Burlington Street. All of the early automobile dealerships were established in downtown Iowa City and nearby areas before their migration away from the central part of the city took place. (FWK.)

The concept of an electric vehicle is not new. This 1920 photograph shows a University of Iowa Hospital bus that ran on battery power. The image was made on Iowa Avenue, across from the 1897 hospital. (FWK.)

This 1947 photograph shows a brand new DeSoto Custom Suburban Sedan, outfitted as a university hospital ambulance. For a time, the university operated a large fleet of ambulances. (FWK.)

On August 13, 1904, the CRANDIC interurban electric railway opened, utilizing an overhead electric wire connection. Running one car at a time, it was primarily a passenger line, but also conveyed some freight. The cars made as many as 60 stops between Cedar Rapids and Iowa City. Some of the trains could top 80 miles per hour. The town of Swisher, along the rail line, was also created in 1904. In Iowa City, the CRANDIC ended by making a circle around the present-day Old Capitol Center. On one memorable day in November 1922, with a football game taking place at the university when dirt roads became quagmires after an intensive rain event, the rail line rescued many stranded motorists. The CRANDIC saw ebbs and flows in ridership over the years, and finally ended passenger service on May 30, 1953. Among the last passengers was Alfred N. Scales of Iowa City, who had also ridden the first train in 1904. In this c. 1915 photograph, a CRANDIC car is seen on the overpass at Riverside Drive in Iowa City. (FWK.)

When the CRANDIC began service in 1904, there was also talk of having a streetcar (trolley) in Iowa City. Willard Main proposed a streetcar line through his new East Iowa City when he platted it in 1899. But it was the Rundell Land and Improvement Company that promised a streetcar line if enough lots were sold in the new Rundell Addition. After 80 lots were sold, the Iowa City Electric Railway Company was organized, and the first streetcar ran on November 17, 1910. Eventually, five different lines were established, with the company initially maintaining one-half-hour service. Like the CRANDIC, the streetcars ran using overhead electric lines. The initial fares were 5¢, also the price of a scoop of ice cream or a coke at a local drugstore. One man served each car as both motorman and conductor. The streetcars had a relatively short life of 21 years. With the advent of the "go anywhere" bus, with the ability to traverse a much larger area, the streetcar system ended in 1931. This c. 1910s photograph shows two streetcars on Dubuque Street alongside Hotel Jefferson. In the background, above the trailing car, the conical dome of Close Hall on Iowa Avenue can be seen. (FWK.)

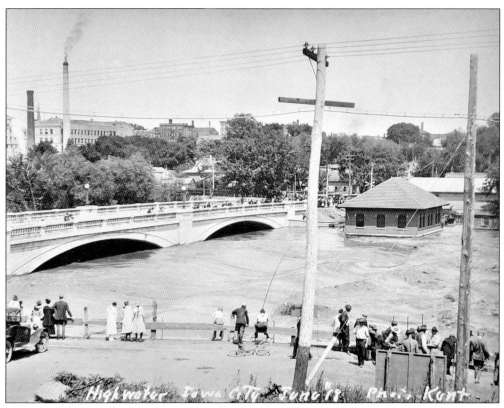

This 1918 photograph shows the raging floodwaters of the Iowa River at the Burlington Street Bridge. Low-lying areas on the east bank of the river, including many houses, were flooded. It was the highest water since the flood of 1881, left Iowa City without power or light, caused great damage to crops, and created a backup of Ralston Creek with flooding in the center of the city. (FWK.)

The Park Road Bridge is shown during the 1918 flood, with water reaching almost over the bridge's road surface. The streetcar was on the line that crossed the bridge into Manville Heights. (FWK.)

The 1918 flood left Iowa Field under eight feet of water, rendering the baseball diamond useless. After the damage was repaired, football resumed in the fall at the south end of the field. (FWK.)

The 2006 tornado that swept through the central part of the city did considerable damage, but thankfully, it did not have a very wide swath. The destruction seen here is along Iowa Avenue. (Iowa City Public Library.)

This c. 1925 view is looking west on Washington Street from the Dubuque Street intersection. Three competing modes of transportation are seen, with the automobile featured most prominently. Gone are the horses and buggies. The streetcar, which plied five routes in town until 1931, was replaced after only a 21-year run by the "go anywhere" bus, of which three can be seen in this image. An officer is seen directing traffic. The Jefferson Hotel, built in 1913, received an extra two stories in 1928. Racine's No. 2, seen on the awning at the hotel, was one of four Racine cigar, billiards, and candy outlets concurrently in business. (FWK.)

The Town Pump service station opened in 1930, announcing that "after being formally opened, keys will be thrown away, as the station will be open day and night every day in the year." It was located on Linn Street, where Hotel Vetro stands today. (FWK.)

Dean Jones began in the oil business in 1932, opened a facility at the corner of Burlington and Madison Streets in 1941, and built this new facility over the old one in 1948. With a staff of 22, it included a complete service area, offices, and a showroom to show off four of his new Hudson cars. Jones also had the distributorship for Texaco and General Tires. During the formal opening, a free Texaco Fire Chief hat was given to each child accompanied by an adult. Ladies could avail themselves of a powder room done in two-toned pink. Jones later expanded his business to sell used cars. Before November 1958, US Highway 6 coursed through downtown Iowa City along Burlington Street, until a bypass was built on the south edge of the city. However, even into the 1960s, a remarkable 14 service stations dotted a six-block stretch of downtown Burlington Street. In 1970, the University of Iowa's new Lindquist Center was constructed on this site. (FWK.)

In the early days of aviation, there were no navigation aids to help pilots find their way at night. In the early 1920s, the US Postal Service worked to complete a system of beacons with towers spaced 15 to 25 miles apart. Seen here in 1925, is one such beacon, at Iowa City's Smith Field with a biplane for mail transport at left. (FWK.)

In this undated photograph, outside the "United Hanger" at the Iowa City Municipal Airport is a DC-3, the first commercially successful airliner. It became legendary and was converted to military use in World War II as the C47. United Air Lines served Iowa City until 1959 and Ozark Air Lines until 1972. Commercial passenger service is no longer available in Iowa City. (FWK.)

The Coralville Dam was constructed by the US Army Corps of Engineers and completed in 1958, primarily for flood control on the Mississippi River. Naively, Iowa City permitted the development of Parkview Terrace ("Mosquito Flats") and other nearby land but lost the gamble when the spillway of the dam was breached as Iowa City flooded in 1993 and again in 2008. After a buyout program, many or most of the homes in Parkview Terrace were demolished. This photograph was taken during the construction of the dam. (US Army Corps of Engineers.)

The Iowa City Water Service Company was privately owned until 1961, when it became municipal. At that time, only three Iowa cities had privately held water companies. In 1972, Iowa City installed what was believed to be the first successful fully computerized surface water plant in the world, utilizing an all-pressure system. The operation control center is pictured in this 1972 photograph. On the wall at left is the diagram of the treatment process; in the center, the filtration system; and at right, the operation of the four water storage tanks distributed throughout the city. This system functioned until 2003, when a new water treatment and distribution plant opened north of Interstate 80. Unlike the old system, which took water directly from the Iowa River, the new plant processes water taken primarily from riverbank alluvial deposits. (Iowa City Water Department.)

Four

THE UNIVERSITY

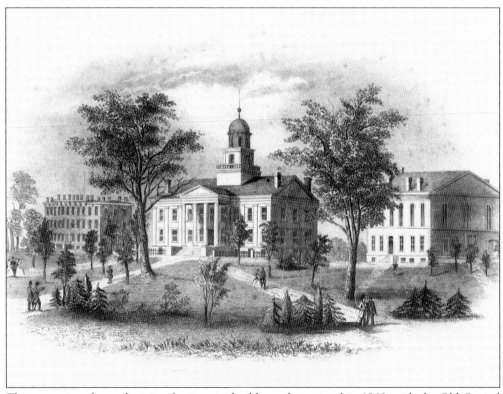

This engraving shows the trio of university buildings that existed in 1869, with the Old Capitol as the "Central Building." After the capital was moved to Des Moines in 1857, Old Capitol was given over to the university. To its left is South Hall, built in 1863 as the first building constructed specifically for the university. It was followed by North Hall at right in 1866. The buildings each housed many departments of the university over their life spans. South Hall was lost in a 1901 fire, and North Hall was razed in 1949. (FWK.)

European-born and trained Gustavus Detlef Hinrichs (1836–1923) was a sparkplug in early University history. A man of boundless energy, he argued for a strong Iowa City high school to properly educate prospective University of Iowa students. He helped get North Hall built, contributed to the definition of the Periodic Table of the Chemical Elements, named the straight-line winds phenomenon "derecho," and organized perhaps the first state weather reporting agency in the country. His domineering, self-righteous attitudes and antagonistic tactics, however, eventually led to his dismissal from the university. He went on to St. Louis University, where he was a professor until his retirement in 1907.

Reunions are a way of staying connected and renewing friendships. In this 1910 photograph, the University of Iowa class of 1876 is pictured on the steps of the Old Capitol during one such reunion. (FWK.)

Built in 1890 with a boost from Helen Close, Close Hall opened as a YMCA/YWCA. The first-ever college basketball game with five players on each side was played here in January 1896, when the University of Iowa invited student-athletes from the new University of Chicago for an experimental game. The final score was Chicago 15, Iowa 12. Close Hall became the home of the journalism program of the university and the *Daily Iowan* newspaper. After a 1940 fire, Close Hall remained as a one-story structure until demolished in 1970. (FWK.)

Members of the University of Iowa band are seen here when the military department of the university staged an annual march and encampment at Camp Carroll in West Liberty. Two battalions left Iowa City at different times and a mock attack was made on the battalion that established a defensive position. The 18-mile trek followed Lower Muscatine Road for almost the entire distance. The four-day event, which included dress parades, lectures, competitive drills, and a band concert, attracted crowds of spectators. (FWK.)

When lightning struck North Hall in 1897, the building held the largest academic library west of the Mississippi River, and almost all of the 27,500 books were lost. Iowa City firefighter Lycurgus Leek lost his life, the first such loss in Iowa City firefighting history. Despite pleas for the state to fund the construction of a fireproof building, North Hall was repaired and the library was once again established there. It took until 1941 for the legislature to fund a new library building.

After the university finally constructed a dedicated library building, the first unit opened in 1951. A long human chain has been formed to effect the transfer of books into the new facility. The light-colored car at left appears to be a 1949 Studebaker. (FWK.)

In this 1920s image, Bohumil Shimek is seen guiding two students in a botany experiment. Shimek graduated with a degree in civil engineering but turned to the natural sciences and taught at the University of Iowa for over 40 years. He was recognized internationally as a naturalist and contributor to the field of botany. Iowa's Shimek State Forest and Iowa City's Shimek Elementary School are named for him. (FWK.)

When Science Hall was only 20 years old, a decision was made to build a new natural sciences building where Science Hall stood. After professors Samuel Calvin and Thomas Macbride petitioned to save the building from destruction, a Chicago firm was contracted to move the building across Jefferson Street, turn it, and place it on a new foundation. Employed in the move were 800 jack screws, 675 six-inch, four-foot rollers, and 27 boxcar loads of timbers. During its three-month move, classes continued throughout the process "without even a test tube being upset, or a crack in the building." (SC.)

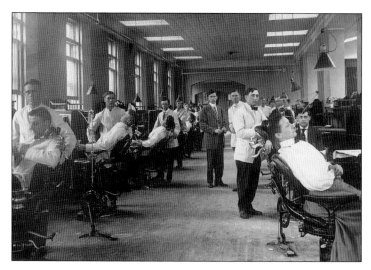

This c. 1900 photograph shows a student dental clinic at the university. Two foot-powered dental drills are seen in the foreground, as well as a hand-held cuspidor at the far left. This image was probably made in "Old Dental," which served dentistry from 1895 until 1918. When a new building opened, cuspidors with running water and electrically driven drills were introduced. (FWK.)

From 1918 to 1973 the College of Dentistry was housed in Trowbridge Hall. Seen here is the massive clinic floor known as the infirmary, consisting of 140 patient treatment areas that would not pass the test for the privacy concerns of today. Each space had a beautiful wooden cabinet. On icy days, the students would observe cars sliding down the adjacent Market Street hill, providing a form of "entertainment." (FWK.)

This building on the corner of Iowa Avenue and Clinton Street was the St. James Hotel before briefly serving as the Iowa Union. The University Book Store and Fink's Cigar Store occupied the ground floor when this photograph was taken in 1915. A 1916 fire destroyed the building and it was replaced by a two-story structure that survives today. (FWK.)

University High School was established in 1916. This 1926 photograph shows a typing class. The male student at left is seen transcribing from a Dictaphone near the edge of his desk. (FWK.)

Currier Residence Hall, the oldest extant university residence hall, is seen in 1928. It was built for female students in 1914, housing 168 students that year, and it is now coeducational. (FWK.)

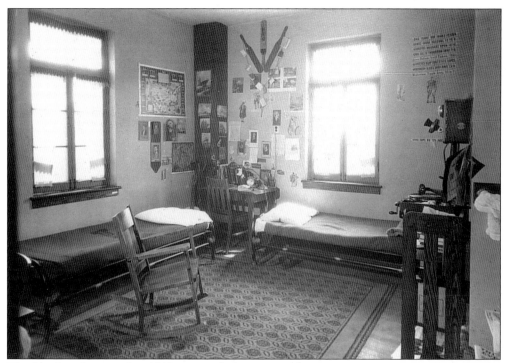

The Quadrangle opened in 1920 as a men's dormitory. This 1920s image portrays a typical room with simple cot-like beds, a wall-mounted telephone, and even a Victrola-type record player, seen at right. The "Quad" closed in 2016 and was razed, and a new College of Pharmacy building now occupies the site. (FWK.)

A trio of law students are shown relaxing in the law commons in this 1948 photograph. The large console radio in its beautiful cabinet offers news and entertainment before the dawn of the television age. (FWK.)

A group of six women students is pictured watching a small black-and-white television screen in 1959 in a lounge in Currier Residence Hall. (FWK.)

This c. 1900 image is illustrative of the classroom technology of the day. A "magic lantern" projector used a light bulb, a focusing mirror, and a glass slide. In the 20th century, Carousel-type projectors evolved but gave way to electronic projection in the 21st century. This dentistry classroom also utilized a blackboard and a giant model of an upper dental arch as instructional aids. (FWK.)

Prof. Dean Kay is seen lecturing to his geology class in this 1930s photograph, with an amazing assortment of rocks seen at right. (FWK.)

The MECCA parade float in this 1920 parade is promoting the effort to build a union at the university. MECCA parades were the highlight of MECCA week, which was held for many years and organized by engineering students. (FWK.)

This MECCA parade float celebrates the laying of the cornerstone of the new Iowa Memorial Union in 1923. Behind it at left is the Berkeley Imperial Hotel and at right, a "Rent-A-Ford, Drive It" garage. After World War I, student unions honoring veterans of that war and earlier ones were being constructed at a number of large Midwestern universities. (FWK.)

The 1898 Iowa football team is shown here with a backdrop of the line of Pentacrest buildings. Protective equipment was meager, and the two-platoon system had not yet come into use, so the same athletes played both offense and defense. The physical demands of the game were rigorous. (FWK.)

Iowa tackle Duke Slater, who played between 1918 and 1921, was Iowa's first black All-American football player. He went on to obtain a law degree and served as a judge. The university's Slater Hall and Slater Field are named for him. (FWK.)

Nile Kinnick is seen crouching with a hand raised while conferring with Coach Eddie Anderson, in preparation for the Iowa-Notre Dame game in November 1939. Standing are Al Coupee, Ed McLain, and Ray Murphy. Iowa defeated Notre Dame and finished the season with six wins, one tie, and one loss, gaining the nickname of the "Ironmen." Kinnick, a halfback, won the coveted Heisman Trophy in 1939 but tragically was killed while on a naval training flight in 1943. (FWK.)

In this undated photograph, Iowa football players are being inspired to beat Notre Dame again, with reminders that the Irish were defeated 7-6 in 1939 and 7-0 in 1940, when Notre Dame was ranked seventh in the United States. (FWK.)

The University of Iowa Elementary School opened in the fall of 1915, using "three especially qualified elementary school teachers," who were supervised by Dr. Ernest Horn, for whom an Iowa City elementary school is named. After its beginning in Schaeffer Hall, the program moved to Old Dental in 1917 and then to North Hall, north of the Pentacrest, in 1925. In this 1925 photograph, students are observed churning butter. The elementary school teaching staff used innovative methods with a faculty consisting mostly of university graduate students. (FWK.)

A group of young children is supervised by university staff in this wonderful photograph from the 1920s. The little girl at lower left is holding on to her friend, while the staff hold a variety of reading materials. (FWK.)

The Old Capitol received a major remodeling in the early 1920s after it was found to be sinking at its foundation and exhibiting other ill effects. Here, mechanical advantage is shown by the use of numerous jacks to prop the building back up. (FWK.)

As part of the interior work of the 1920s Old Capitol reconstruction, the amazing spiral staircase was rebuilt, as shown in this 1923 photograph. (FWK.)

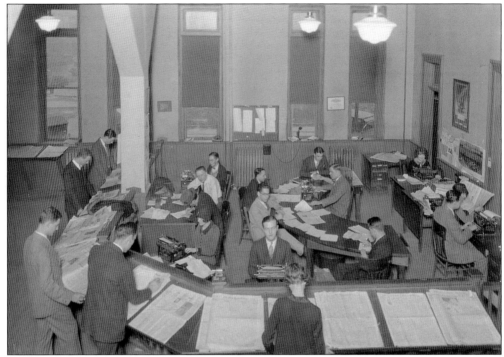

This 1925 photograph illustrates the complexity involved with the production of the *Daily Iowan*. Each person, whether seated or standing, is kept on task. At this time, the newspaper office was in Close Hall on Iowa Avenue. (FWK.)

The long-running *Daily Iowan* University of Iowa student newspaper began its life in 1868 as the *University Reporter*, later becoming the *Vidette-Reporter*. A woman is seen here reading in Close Hall with a bewildering array of papers folded as well as tacked onto boards. (FWK.)

Students are shown in a 1920s university drafting class. When computer-aided design programs were launched in the late 1900s, this methodology, along with mechanical calculators and slide rules, became only a distant memory. (FWK.)

In this c. 1930s image, students are using 100-key manual calculators. After the information was entered, a lever on the right side of the machine was turned to perform the calculation. The instructor, seen in the background, appears to be tabulating the results. Little did they know that a tiny hand-held electronic device with far more power would one day replace these cumbersome machines. (FWK.)

The College of Pharmacy dates to 1885, with Iowa City pharmacist and industrialist Emil Boerner as its first dean. In the early days of pharmacy, compounding was more prevalent than it is today. This 1930s photograph pictures a student in a laboratory. (FWK.)

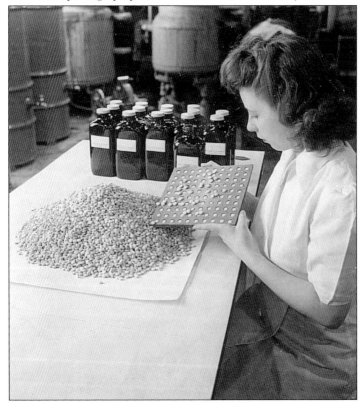

This 1940s photograph is of a student tasked with the tedious process of sorting a large inventory of pills. (FWK.)

A young George Gallup is pictured here in 1924. He played football at the University of Iowa, was an editor of the *Daily Iowan* newspaper, and received his PhD in 1928. As a pioneer of survey sampling techniques and inventor of the Gallup poll, he suffered a moment of embarrassment when he predicted that Dewey would defeat Truman in the 1948 presidential election. (FWK.)

The Wendell Johnson Speech and Hearing Center is seen in this 1960s photograph. Wendell Johnson was a pioneer in the field of speech pathology, including stuttering, and spent most of his career on the faculty of the University of Iowa. He was also instrumental in the founding of the American Speech and Hearing Association. (FWK.)

The first annual induction ceremony at the University of Iowa was held in 1921, with a mile-long parade. These events continued for decades. In the October 1, 1924, parade pictured here, a long procession of students and officials is seen looping along Iowa Avenue. As part of the ceremony, this would be recited: "I pledge, here and now, lifelong loyalty to the ideals of scholarship and character of the founders of this institution, to the end that I may loyally serve this university, this commonwealth, and this nation." (FWK.)

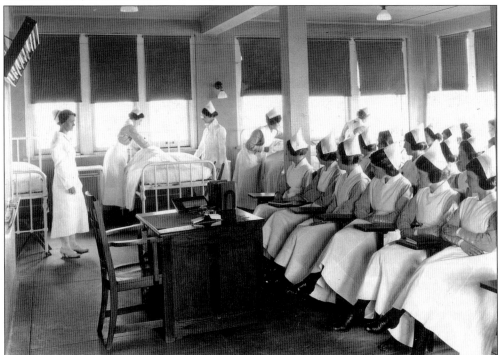

The University of Iowa nursing class seen in this 1920s photograph appears to be focused on the manner of making up patients' beds. The uniforms of the day are in stark contrast to today's much less formal attire. (FWK.)

E.F. Lindquist (left) and Ted McCarrel are seen in this 1950s photograph alongside the first optical mark reading machine at the University of Iowa. Lindquist introduced the Iowa Test of Basic Skills for elementary and middle school students in 1935. Later programs followed, with Lindquist becoming highly respected in the field of educational measurement. Drawing in part on these testing programs, Lindquist and McCarrel developed the American College Testing Program (ACT) with the goal of testing broad competencies rather than testing for rote memorization, after finding that previous college entrance testing programs were both meager and fragmented. The two men partnered with others, both locally and nationally, to quickly develop the first test and enlist participation. The first administration of the test was on Saturday, November 7, 1959, to over 75,000 students, covering a widespread area of the United States. The ACT quickly took root and became a major competitor to the Scholastic Aptitude Test (SAT), which was introduced in 1926. ACT became a major employer in Iowa City. (FWK.)

Dr. Ignacio Ponseti was born in Mallorca and received a doctor of medicine degree in 1936 at the University of Barcelona. He completed his residency in orthopedic surgery at the University of Iowa and had a broad background in the basic sciences, including molecular biology and a whole range of orthopedic surgical conditions. He is best known for his nonsurgical treatment of club foot, which won him universal acclaim. He is seen here in 1942 at the age of 28 at the Iowa City Rock Island Depot with an unidentified man. (Dr. Ponseti Papers, Special Collections and Archives, the University of Iowa Libraries.)

Celebrated physicist James Van Allen is shown here in 1953 in his laboratory, holding a space probe. He figured prominently in the early manned space program, discovered a radiation belt around the Earth that would bear his name, and had the honor of a new physics building named for him during his lifetime. An elementary school in North Liberty, Iowa, is also named for him. (FWK.)

A one-of-a-kind bagpipe band, the Scottish Highlanders, was formed through the ROTC department at the University of Iowa in 1937 and became an all-girls band during World War II. They performed at football games and were invited to appear across the nation and even internationally, being at one time the largest bagpipe band in the world. The University of Iowa dissolved the organization in 2008. (FWK.)

Grant Wood is seen here c. 1940, seated at left in a mural studio at the University of Iowa. Wood is best known for his world-famous 1930 oil on beaverboard, *American Gothic*. For a number of years before his untimely death in 1942, Wood lived in the 1850s home on Court Street built by pioneer brickmaker Nicholas Oakes. (FWK.)

To some, the card catalogs seen in this c. 1972 photograph represent a time warp. Today's youngsters would not even recognize it. Online access to the information within this vast depository makes for convenience, but there was a significant outlay of time to effect the changeover. (FWK.)

In this 1960s photograph are shown five men associated with the University of Iowa's Writers' Workshop. All of them made their mark in various fields of writing. They are, from left to right, Edmund Keeley, Mark Strand, Vance Bourjaily, R.V. Cassill, and Paul Engle. (FWK.)

In this 1950s photograph, Paul Engle is seen conducting a class. Engle was a longtime director of the Writers' Workshop, the oldest writing program in the United States offering a master of fine arts degree. (FWK.)

Philip Hubbard, at right, is seen here conferring with Dr. John Peoples, President of Jackson State University, on an unknown date. When Hubbard enrolled at the University of Iowa, African Americans were not allowed in dormitories. He became the first black faculty member at Iowa, worked promoting civil rights, and became the first black administrator in Iowa's state university system. Hubbard Park was named for him in 1990. (Philip G. Hubbard Papers, Special Collections and Archives, the University of Iowa Libraries.)

In 1913, a home economics department was founded at the University of Iowa. The course of study included the study of foods, textiles, sanitation, the home, the making of clothing, dietetics, and household management. The curriculum was later expanded to include such things as child care, marriage and family relations, family economics, and the printing and dying of fabrics. The program was closed in the early 1990s. This November 22, 1944, photograph shows a group of home economics students and staff. (FWK.)

Five

WORSHIP AND LEISURE

Old Brick, built as the First Presbyterian Church in the mid-1800s, was constructed on land donated by city founder Chauncey Swan. After a new church was built on the east side of town, Old Brick was retained as a performance and meeting venue. (SC.)

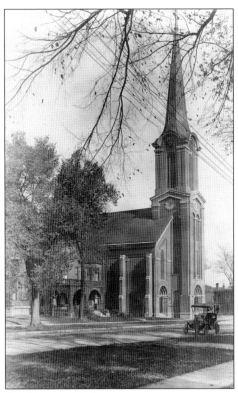

This c. 1920 photograph shows the 1868 St. Mary's Church on Jefferson Street. The church was built around an existing one, and when the exterior walls of the new church were completed, the old church was dismantled and removed through the front doors of the new church. (FWK.)

The Bethel African Methodist Episcopal Church was built in 1868 on South Governor Street, outside of the city limits, because African Americans were not permitted to own property within the city. This is Iowa City's only historically black church. (A.)

Prominent in this early-1900s photograph is the 1868 First Congregational Church. The conical top of the Methodist church can be seen just to the left. At far left is the St. Mary's school and private residences are seen at right. The university would eventually take over the entire block at right, save for the church. (SC.)

The Trinity Episcopal congregation was organized in 1853 and after worshiping in a variety of locations, the cornerstone for this building was laid in 1871. The original part of the structure is seen in this c. 1915 photograph. The cost, including the lots, was about $12,000. After expansion, this section remains today, somewhat belying its age. (FWK.)

Nurseryman P.J. Regan developed his "Minnehaha" resort north of Iowa City on the north bank of the Iowa River in 1898 and built the first Iowa City golf course on the grounds in 1900. To bring patrons in, Regan offered steamboat excursions two days a week and his "band wagon," which ran multiple hours on certain days. The golf course later became that of the Iowa City Country Club, and in 1947, the country club property along with its clubhouse and golf course, about 120 acres, were purchased by the Iowa City Elks Lodge. (Special Collections, University of Iowa Libraries.)

This 1914 image captures a chess game using humans as chess pieces. It took place on old Iowa Field on the east side of the Iowa River. The "Iowa Fights" sign is featured prominently and the base of the stands appears to be adorned with a set intended for some sort of skit. (FWK.)

106

The university baseball diamond was at the north end of Iowa Field on the east bank of the Iowa River, between Burlington Street and Iowa Avenue. This c. 1895 photograph shows spectators seated on the bare ground and standing, with their horses and carriages nearby. Grandstands would be added later. In the background at the top of the image are the five largest buildings on the Pentacrest. Gold Medal flour, introduced in 1880 and now a product of General Mills, is advertised on a building at center left. The many homes seen on the other side of the fence would be gone by the 1920s. (SC.)

This 1925 aerial photograph looking north shows Iowa Field and the baseball diamond, occupying the entire east side river bank between Burlington Street and Iowa Avenue. After the new football stadium was built in 1929, this area became a parking lot with the English-Philosophy Building later constructed at the north end. (FWK.)

In this 1907 photograph, the Gollmar Brothers Circus troupe is shown parading south on Dubuque Street at the corner of Washington Street. Included were many brass bands, a steam calliope, open dens of animals, riders dressed in costumes and mounted on Arabian steeds, Roman chariots drawn by Shetland ponies, elephants, camels, hippopotami, and dromedaries. The 1876 corner building housing Thomas Hardware still stands, where Raygun occupies the ground floor. At right is Reichardt's Café, known for its handmade candies and ice creams. Between the 1870s and 1950s, numerous circuses played at Iowa City, including those of the Ringling Brothers, Barnum and Bailey's Greatest Show on Earth, and others, using at least two different grounds. (Margaret Hibbs.)

The man that put the move in moving pictures in Iowa City

Thomas A. (Buster) Brown
Proprietor and Manager
BROWN'S SMOKE HOUSE, 24 Clinton St.
BROWN'S AMERICAN, 124 Washington St.
BROWN'S NICKELDOM, 128 Washington St.

Thomas "Buster" Brown was a pioneer in the Iowa City movie business. He operated Brown's Nickeldom as "the coolest spot in Iowa City and the only 5c show in the world with a 20-piece orchestra." His theater ran from about 1907 to 1913, with electric fans and opera chairs. He also owned the American Theatre and, for a time, was a tobacconist with *Brown's Smoke House*. (Special Collections, University of Iowa Libraries.)

This beautiful theatrical poster announced the 1925 film *The Wedding Song* playing at the Pastime Theatre for three days in February. Opened in 1912, the Pastime, located on College Street on the current Graduate Hotel property, was the first dedicated movie theater built in Iowa City, with the Englert opening later in that year. (Margaret Hibbs.)

Pictured here is the 1917–1918 Iowa City High School basketball team. Most of the players can be seen wearing knee supports. Belts and tank tops distinguish the uniforms from those of today and period teams did not have much depth. (Margaret Hibbs.)

This is a November 1955 photograph of the University of Iowa basketball team. Under coach Bucky O'Connor, the team compiled a 20-6 record during the 1955-1956 season, including 17 consecutive wins, to win its second straight Big Ten title. The squad went on to a second consecutive trip to the Final Four but fell to the unbeaten San Francisco Dons in the title game. The 1979-1980 team also made a trip to the Final Four under coach Lute Olsen. (FWK.)

A football ticket booth is seen in this 1913 photograph. The booth is adjacent to Old Iowa Field, between Iowa Avenue and Burlington Street on the east bank of the Iowa River. The Old Armory is in the background. (FWK.)

In the 1920s, season passes for all university sporting events were issued for a base fee. However, to obtain choice reserved seats, people waited at Whetstone's Drug Store. The caption for this Frederick Kent image reads, "Waiting for Tickets," but mayhem seems to prevail, with blocked cars and almost everyone gazing to the right for undisclosed reasons. (FWK.)

For football fans who were not in attendance at a stadium, a device called the Grid Graph was developed during the 1920s. Electric lights were turned on as information about the plays "came over the wire" (telegraph). This photograph captures a scene in the Iowa Memorial Union in 1926. (FWK.)

Unlike the colorful, casual black-and-gold dress of today, scarcely a man without a hat, coat, or tie can be found in this 1921 football crowd. Women are greatly outnumbered. Close inspection reveals several men smoking cigars and pipes. (FWK.)

A Corner of the Camp Ground

Before the era of radio and television, Chautauqua programs offered learning and entertainment opportunities. Traveling troupes played circuits throughout Iowa and other states, with Iowa leading the nation in the number of programs held in 1920. Iowa City staged programs from 1906 until 1928, often featuring national figures such as William Jennings Bryan and Clarence Darrow. (Special Collections, University of Iowa Libraries.)

After speaking at Iowa City's 1910 Chautauqua, firebrand Carrie Nation held the crowd captive, unable to leave the tent in the rain, and she sold every pin, each cut into the shape of a hatchet. Nation, 63 years old, just delivered her lecture on "how I smashed the saloon, why I smashed the saloon, and how you can smash the saloon." Her wish came true when Iowa went for prohibition in January 1916, four years ahead of national prohibition.

The long-standing women's field hockey program at the University of Iowa has enjoyed much success. Prior to 1973, the program was classified as a "club sport," and since 1973, a varsity sport. The team has won 16 conference championships, six Big Ten titles, and an NCAA championship in 1986. This c. 1910s photograph captures the team in its early days. (University of Iowa Department of Physical Education for Women records, Iowa Women's Archives, University of Iowa Libraries, Iowa City Iowa.)

In this 1911 photograph, freshmen and sophomores are seen playing a game on Iowa Field, using brute force to push a giant six- or eight-foot diameter leather ball over the opponent's goal line. The game was contrived as a method to combat the hazing practices that the university wished to counter. (FWK.)

In this 1920 photograph, a group of "yell leaders" are pictured. Although gone from the University of Iowa, the designation of yell leader carries on in other institutions to this day; for example, with the Texas Aggies. (FWK.)

This 1956 photograph shows a huge version of the university mascot, Herky. An unidentified cheerleader is pretending to pin a badge on the iconic mascot that was "hatched" in 1948. (FWK.)

Jimmy has smoked for seventy-one years.
Why not join his class?

Pipes, Tobacco, Candies and Smoker's Accessories

DISTRIBUTORS OF

Flor De Jeitles, 5c Cigar
La Meloda,   10c Cigar

A. R. Kirk Cigar Store

Successor to Purcell Brothers

This advertisement from the 1917 *Hawkeye* yearbook promotes the sale of cigars at the A. R. Kirk Cigar Store at 116 East Washington Street, declaring and asking, "Jimmy has smoked for seventy-one years. Why not join his class?" "Archie" Kirk was "one of the greatest tackles the Big Nine conference ever boasted . . . and was coach of the football eleven at Simpson College," according to from the *Johnson County Independent*, January 27, 1916. (University of Iowa, Special Collections.)

In this 1940s photograph, a young lady was caught in a whimsical gesture of lighting a young man's cigarette. At the time, the ramifications of cigarette smoking were largely unacknowledged. (FWK.)

117

This 1924 photograph shows WSUI radio station director Carl Menzer in his studio. Menzer became director of the newly licensed station in 1923 and held that position for the next 45 years. He was also involved with experimental television broadcasting in the 1930s. (FWK.)

This 1930 photograph shows equipment that was part of the WSUI radio remote control operation. (FWK.)

In this 1924 photograph, a group of radio performers is shown, along with their piano accompanist and mentor Prof. William Raymond.

When radio reigned as an entertainment medium of the 1930s, a play is shown being broadcast by WSUI in this 1931 photograph. Various sound effects enhanced the production. (FWK.)

In the late 1800s, three competing breweries existed along a one-block stretch of Market Street. This 1917 photograph shows a parade moving eastward on Market Street at the Gilbert Street intersection with the former buildings of the Great Western Brewery at right. The Englert Brewery ceased operations in 1883, but the other two breweries endured until Iowa prohibition took effect in 1916. (FWK.)

After the Englert Theatre opened in late 1912, the Coldren Opera House on Clinton Street could no longer compete and went out of business. In this 1910s photograph, the Englert is prominent, along with the 1910 Paul-Helen Building at right. The sign for the Iowa City Gas and Electric Company, a longtime tenant in Paul-Helen, is at far right. (FWK.)

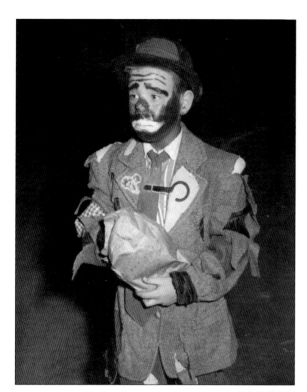

Nine-year-old Dan Keeley put on a sober face in his portrayal of Weary Willie, Emmet Kelley's famous character, while participating in a Scout-O-Rama in Iowa City in 1958. (David Keeley.)

Jerry Neuzil, at about age five, is seen here in about 1946, preparing to "run away" from home, complete with a suitcase and wearing a woman's high-laced shoes. He was known throughout his neighborhood near Kinnick Stadium, always wearing a smile. He parked cars for football fans for 5¢. (Virginia Neuzil Kleis.)

The newly-built 18-hole university golf course is seen in the mid-1950s, almost completely barren of trees. Today, boasting hundreds of mature trees, Finkbine is one of the best public courses in the state. University Heights is near the top center and temporary barracks buildings for married student housing can be seen in two nearby locations at upper left. Robert Finkbine's sons W.O. and E.C. became wealthy through the lumber business and donated land in the early 1920s for the first university golf course, located to the north, and dedicated it to their father. This first course was retained in part as "Lower Finkbine" after the new course was opened. W.O. also helped fund the Iowa Memorial Union, founded an annual dinner to honor prominent student leaders, and is a namesake for the annual Hancher-Finkbine Medallion awarded to outstanding individuals. (FWK.)

Shown here in January 1964 is the first show given by the Old Capitol Chorus, a men's barbershop singing group. Director Glenn Jablonski and chorus members are striking sober poses. SPEBSQSA stands for the Society for the Preservation and Encouragement of Barbershop Quartet Singing in America, Incorporated, founded in 1938, a title in playful mockery of the names of government agencies of the Roosevelt administration. Old Capitol has had over 450 boys and men go through its ranks. Women's barbershop in Iowa City also has a long history in Iowa City with a group now known as Metro Mix. (Old Capitol Chorus.)

This undated photograph shows the cast of an Iowa City Community Theatre production of *Oklahoma!* Community Theatre is the longest-standing amateur theatrical group in Iowa City. It owes its 1956 start to a University of Iowa student who wrote a play and to get it produced enlisted Frank Morrison to form a nucleus of persons who then began the theater. It was originally affiliated with the Iowa City Recreation Commission, from which it received secretarial aid and sponsorship. Numerous other theatrical groups, both community and university, have a presence today. (Iowa City Community Theatre.)

This 1930s photograph shows a large crowd attending a billiards exhibition at the Iowa Memorial Union. (FWK.)

This image of a 1950 dance party conjures up thoughts of bobby socks, saddle shoes, and sock hops. All of the women are wearing long skirts. Perhaps the young man has a "dance card" in his back pocket. (FWK.)

This 1960s photograph shows an unidentified University of Iowa School of Religion faculty in front of the Agudas Achim (Association of Brothers) Synagogue. (FWK.)

This 1910s photograph shows a group of men in the Unitarian Church reading room. The church was constructed in 1908 and served the congregation until a new church was built in Coralville. The 1908 structure was repurposed. (FWK.)

In this charming 1938 photograph, a woman has captured the attention of three young boys, as she lets the one at left produce sound with a bow against the violin. (FWK.)

In 1963, Doris Preucil began instructing young children in violin by a method developed by Japanese violinist Shinichi Suzuki. After teaching students for a number of years in her home, Doris and her husband, William, opened their Preucil School of Music in 1975 and the nonprofit music school endures after almost 50 years, serving students ages three through adult at two locations. Doris is shown here instructing Carmel Ray. (Doris and William Preucil.)

In this 1968 photograph, 14-year-old Mike Hotka, sponsored by the Iowa-Illinois Gas and Electric Company, is seated in his home-built soapbox derby entry car for the July Iowa City event. Boys 11 to 15 years old were eligible, provided car and driver weights did not exceed 250 pounds and all cars used the same axles and wheels. Girls were first allowed to compete in the Iowa City race in 1971. Iowa City races were held from 1943 to 1972. (Phil Hotka.)

This 1950s photograph shows a number of women members of an unidentified University of Iowa sorority with their house mother seated at the right. (FWK.)

Six

BUSINESS AND COMMUNITY

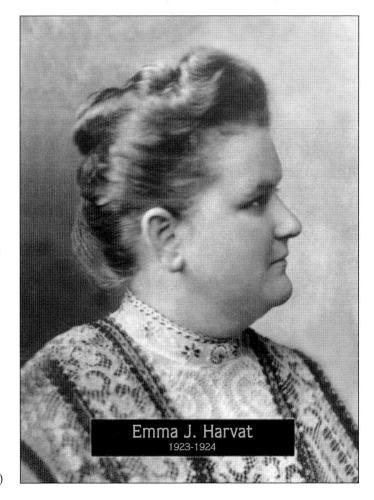

Successful businesswoman Emma Harvat was Iowa City's first female mayor, serving in the early 1920s. She was the first female holder of an aldermanic post in Iowa City and believed to be the first female mayor of a city in the United States with a population over 10,000. Her election captured the attention of national and international newspapers. The Iowa City Council chambers are named for Harvat. (City of Iowa City.)

Emma J. Harvat
1923-1924

Moses Bloom (1833–1893) served in both houses of the Iowa General Assembly, was perhaps the first Jewish mayor of a major American city, and was the first Iowa City Jewish settler. He once served as an Iowa City postmaster and established a manufactory for commercial alcohol production. His 1858 frame building on Clinton Street, later replaced by a brick one, was the site of a long-running clothing store.

The First National Bank is seen in this c. 1910s photograph. It was common for doctors to occupy second-floor space in downtown buildings, and First National had two of them: Dr. Zella W. Stewart and Dr. George Wenzlick. On the left, along North Dubuque Street are Slavata and Eppel Clothiers, later Eppel Clothes Store and the W.P. Hohenschuh Furniture Store. Hohenschuh's father ran a furniture store in Iowa City in the 1850s and both Hohenschuhs were also undertakers. W.P. achieved national stature in the field of mortuary science. Streetcar tracks and associated overhead power lines feature prominently in the image. (SC.)

Kathryn Bartosky was born in Pilsen, Bohemia, in 1850 and came to Johnson County with her parents in 1868. At this time, many Bohemian and German immigrants settled in the area of Iowa City which would receive the moniker of "Goosetown." A sampling of surnames with origins in Goosetown might include Alberhasky, Chadek, Chopek, Hayek, and Cilek. Kathryn Bartosky is seen here in her kitchen, perhaps preparing a batch of donuts, for which she was noted. Until 98 years old, she "turned out huge batches of them for church socials and neighbors." When she died in 1954, she was believed to be Iowa City's oldest resident at age 103. (Virginia Neuzil Kleis.)

Before the advent of modern construction machinery, extensive use of block-and-tackle devices was necessary to hoist heavy materials into place. This 1890s photograph shows the complexity of the procedure. (FWK.)

Strub's may have been the first department store in Iowa City. Begun in the 1860s at 118 South Clinton Street, it became Aldens in 1946 and then Roshek's in 1972, until closing in 1979, having been at the same location for 111 years. (FWK.)

In the early 1900s, Iowa City had a number of laundries, mainly along Iowa Avenue. The circa 1895 C.O.D. Laundry on Iowa Avenue served multiple purposes. The building housed the first Iowa City Public Library, the Iowa City Post Office during its 1930s expansion, and a number of businesses. Today, it serves as a nightclub. (Special Collections, University of Iowa Libraries.)

This 1930 photograph shows the new New Process Laundry, constructed on South Dubuque Street at a cost of $100,000. Equipment included eight washers, four extractors, fifteen air-driven presses, a collar ironer, collar shaper, collar and cuff starcher, sleeve ironer, bosom press, curtain stretcher, dry tumbler, dry room, and flatwork ironer. About 30,000 gallons of soft water were used every day. New Process was in business here until the 1980s. (FWK.)

The 1850s Metropolitan Building is shown burning during an uncontrollable fire in 1912. The fire hoses were incapable of reaching the top story of the building and Iowa City's privately held water company received severe criticism in the press. During the next year, a group of businessmen financed the construction of Hotel Jefferson on the burned-out site. (FWK.)

A number of fire companies were established in the late 1800s, but not until the early 1900s was a department with paid firemen instituted. This c. 1925 image shows the famous team of white Percheron horses, Snowball and Highball, hitched to the fire department's hose wagon. Snowball and Highball served the department from 1912 until 1925. They are posed in front of the 1881 city hall in the 10 block of South Linn Street. Seated left is Mayor H.H. Carroll with Fire Chief James Clark. Standing from left to right are Assistant Chief Herman Amish, Assistant Chief George Kaspar, and firefighters Charles Reizenstein, Raymond Morgan, Albert Dolezal, and Louis Villhauer. (Norwood C. "Bud" Louis.)

The 1881 city hall building shown at left housed the fire department, with equipment behind the three doors at ground level. The small light-colored building at right housed the police department. When the new civic center was built in 1961, both departments were moved, and the old city hall was demolished. (Greg Kruse.)

This c. 1895 photograph shows "Elizabeth Irish's School of Shorthand and Typewriting." Elizabeth, a descendant of Iowa City pioneer Captain Irish, ran her school for 45 years, also operating a placement service for her graduates. She retired in 1940 at 84 years of age. Her motto was "Work and Work and Work and Work." She was the first woman to hold a secretarial position in Iowa City and Johnson County and the only woman member of the Iowa City Commercial Club for 45 years.

The *Iowa City Daily Press*, established in 1841, and the *Iowa City Daily Citizen*, established in 1891 were consolidated in 1920 and began publication as the *Iowa City Press-Citizen* on November 1. It would be an independent newspaper with representation from both political parties. In 1937, the *Press-Citizen* opened this new building constructed in the Art Deco Streamline Moderne style. Today, the building serves as an apartment complex. (FWK.)

The St. Patrick's Catholic School was prominent on the southwest corner of Linn and Court Streets as seen in this 1920s photograph. The associated church across the street suffered catastrophic damage in the 2006 tornado that ripped through the downtown. The church and later the school were both demolished. A hotel and large apartment complex now stand on the former school site. (FWK.)

HOHENSCHUH'S
═══MORTUARY═══

J. H. DONOHUE
Funeral Director and Proprietor

PHONE—Day or Night—1237

HOHENSCHUH MORTUARY

H. S. SAMPLE, Assistant

13-15 S. Linn Street   *Iowa City, Iowa*

W.P. Hohenschuh built his new mortuary on South Linn Street in 1917, as seen in this 1920s advertisement. He was formerly in both the furniture and mortuary business on Dubuque Street. Hohenschuh organized the Iowa Funeral Directors Association, figured prominently in mortuary science colleges, and was a principal figure in the National Funeral Directors' Association. In the late 1920s, at least four Iowa City funeral homes served a population of 15,000, whereas today, only two remain for over 70,000 people. Hohenschuh died in 1920, but his name was so revered that his former funeral business bore his name alone until 1959.

When Northwestern Bell Telephone Company constructed this building in 1929, it was expected to "house repeaters to be installed on the transcontinental toll line" to be built in Iowa City on the way to the Pacific Coast. The building received at least four additions over the years, including an exterior coating of beige-colored pre-cast concrete panels, making today's building unrecognizable from this image. (FWK.)

After returning from New York, where he was schooled in the plumbing trade, William White, seated at right, became part of Connell Bros. & White Plumbing, Heating, and Gas Fitting at 226 South Dubuque Street. White's brother Allen is standing fourth from the left. Workers can be seen seated upon crated sinks and bathtubs in this 1907 photograph. (Bob White.)

In 1929, Montgomery Ward and Company opened an Iowa City store in the 100 block of East College Street. It is shown here just before its February opening with what appears to be well over 100 of its employees. About 150 people were used throughout the opening, and about 75 were kept on after that. The store utilized seven managers. (FWK.)

Despite hopes to keep a major department store downtown as part of the urban renewal process of the 1960s and 1970s, Montgomery Ward made the decision to move in 1966 to a new location with plenty of free parking. The south side shopping center became known as Wardway Plaza. (Margaret Hibbs.)

This MECCA parade was held in the spring of 1920. The "Alcoholic Blues" float was a lament of Prohibition, which began about two months earlier. (FWK.)

The Rinella family established a grocery at the northwest corner of Iowa Avenue and Madison Street in the early 1900s. After all of the structures were removed from that block by the university in the 1920s, the Rinellas established their store here, on Clinton Street, across from the Pentacrest. In 1944, they established the Airliner Restaurant, taking the name from a diner near Midway Airport in Chicago. This c. 1970 photograph shows the establishment, serving as one of 40-some bars in the downtown Iowa City area. (Richard Klinite.)

Whetstones Drug Store at the northeast corner of Clinton and Washington Streets was in business there for just short of a remarkable 100 years. Located adjacent to the university campus, students could cash checks, mail laundry to their homes, and indulge in the famous Persian Sherbet, a secret soda fountain concoction. This 1920s image shows the booths and tables and the prominent soda fountain. Today, the space is occupied by the original Pancheros restaurant. (FWK.)

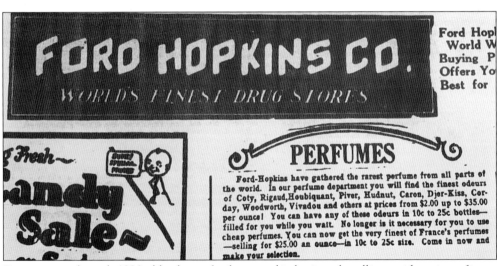

Drugstores in the early 1900s, like those of today, stayed in business by selling a wide variety of items beyond just prescriptions. Competition was often keen, with a large number of stores operating in downtown Iowa City at the same time. Almost all had soda fountains. The Ford Hopkins Company on South Clinton Street lured customers by selling expensive perfumes by a fraction of an ounce. In this 1929 advertisement, 10¢ to 25¢ portions were offered.

Gibbs Drug Store, seen here in 1939, began as Whetstone's Drug Store No. 2 in 1921. Run as Gibbs for 22 years, its building was razed in 1957 to make way for a new Penny's store on the northeast corner of Dubuque and College Streets. In 1939, it was common for merchandise to be in cabinets out of the reach of customers. (FWK.)

In this c. 1947 photograph of Mott's Drug Store, most items are seen to be directly accessible to customers. Mott's, on South Dubuque Street, specialized in newspapers and magazines from around the world and had a small rental library from 1940 to about 1954, from which books could be rented for three days for 10¢. When Charles Mott died in 1988, he had operated his store for 64 years. The store then concentrated on selling fragrances and other non-drug items until closing in 1992. (FWK.)

Lee Nagle moved to Iowa City from Red Oak, Iowa, and, in 1922, opened this lumber yard on West Burlington Street at the site of today's Stanley Museum of Art. The business was moved to South Gilbert Street in 1972. (FWK.)

The Iowa City Poultry and Egg Company was founded in Iowa City in 1923 and, soon after, was doing a half-million dollars' worth of business annually. Between 300 and 400 farmers came to town to sell their chickens and eggs to the company. (FWK.)

Founded in 1896 and incorporated in 1904, Economy Advertising Company may be Iowa City's longest-running business, now located on Highway 6 West. It is seen here around 1928 when it was located in the former brewery building, today's Brewery Square, on Linn Street. A mainstay of the early business was the printing of advertising calendars and other types of printing. (Bill Bywater.)

Smith and Cilek's Hardware Store is represented in this 1910s parade in downtown Iowa City. In 1921, Frank Lenoch bought out Hugh Smith, turning the business into Lenoch and Cilek, a name known to generations of Iowa Citians. The name continues with two Ace hardware stores operating in Iowa City. (Photograph by Julius Hecker, FWK.)

This 1938 photograph shows the Ben Whitebook Grocery on South Dubuque Street. Around this time, there were up to 16 groceries clustered in the downtown area, making one wonder how they could all stay in business. This store was in a building that was razed during urban renewal and is now the site of the north end of Plaza Centre One on the Pedestrian Mall. (FWK.)

This is a 1941 photograph of the interior of the Co-Op Grocery that was established at 210 South Clinton Street in December of that year. When it opened, it was owned by approximately 400 citizens of Iowa City. The store operated on Clinton Street until going out of business in 1956. It was a forerunner of the New Pioneer Co-Op concept of today. (FWK.)

The original part of today's John's Grocery was built as a dry goods store in 1848, but this corner portion came later. Over the years, the building housed a variety of businesses, including many groceries. In 1948, John Alberhasky went into business at this location as John's Grocery, and the store, still in the Alberhasky family, remains the only surviving "mom and pop" in Iowa City.

This drawing depicts Dorrance "Doc" Kehoe outside his People's Grocery on North Dodge Street. Doc and his wife, Guenn, raised their family of five children entirely on the proceeds from their small store, being helped by meat orders from fraternities and sororities. As government regulations tightened and supermarkets came to town, the small groceries were all but gone by the close of the 1990s. (Guenn Kehoe.)

This c. 1940s postcard shows Mercy Hospital before its later major expansion. Mercy and University Hospitals "grew up together" over the years to provide treatment options for area residents. (Margaret Hibbs.)

This 1952 photograph shows the newly completed Veterans Administration Hospital. The hospital has the good fortune to also utilize staff from nearby university hospitals, supplementing treatment regimens for patients. (FWK.)

PATRICIA BEATCH   ROBERT BOTT   LORAIN BRACK   EDWIN CHADEK
SCHARF PHOTO

VIRGINIA COLBERT   LEO CORTIMIGLIA

St. Mary's HIGH SCHOOL Class of 1942

ANNA CORSO   MARIE DONOHOE   PAUL DONAHUE   JOSEPH HALSCH

MAGDALEN LENOCH   THOMAS MAHAN   KATHRYN RUMMELHART   MARGARET SUEPPEL

Many surnames known to long-term Iowa City residents are seen in this photograph of the St. Mary's High School class of 1942. St. Patrick's Catholic Church also operated a high school on Court Street near the downtown. In the fall of 1958, the new Regina Catholic High School was opened. (David Keeley.)

John Nash established an early wholesale grocery business in Iowa City, one which ran for 60 years. In 1962, a flash flood of Ralston Creek devastated his inventory in his warehouse along Burlington Street near today's Robert A. Lee Recreation Center. He is seen here on a trip to Japan where he consulted with some grocer counterparts. (John Nash.)

This 1935 photograph shows Roland Smith's Café on South Dubuque Street. After remodeling later in the year, including the addition of an Art Deco window, Smith's boldly proclaimed itself to be "The finest café in all Iowa." Competition for the downtown restaurant business was strong from other establishments such as Capitol, Hawk's Nest, Marty's, Princess, Reich's, and Pinney's Café, to name but some. After a long career in the restaurant business, Smith went on to an even longer career as a real estate agent, working well past the "normal retirement age," and died at age 96. (FWK.)

Esther Winders was appointed marshal in University Heights in 1952. Colorful and exuberant, she policed the town single-handedly. A university-trained registered nurse, Winders had law enforcement in her blood through family connections. She carried a pearl-handled revolver and patrolled the town on a Harley-Davidson motorcycle by day and in a red Studebaker by night, accompanied by her faithful canine companion, Portia. She appeared on the CBS show *To Tell the Truth* and was featured in a 1969 *Time* magazine article. (David Luck.)

This student protestor was one of many who made a statement against the American involvement in the Vietnam War and in anger toward the Kent State shootings of 1970. Anger turned into violence in May 1971 when windows were broken out in many establishments. (Richard Klinite.)

Archibald Alexander played football and earned an engineering degree from the University of Iowa in 1912, thus breaking through two deeply entrenched color barriers. He formed a company that built freeways, airfields, and power plants and was appointed governor of the US Virgin Islands by President Eisenhower. The Alexander Elementary School in Iowa City is named for him. (Library of Congress.)

The Tate Arms building was constructed in 1940, and Elizabeth Tate ran it as a boardinghouse for young African American men who were denied entry to university dormitories. Strict but fair, she was respected by her boarders. An alternative high school in Iowa City is named for Tate. Helen Lemme also provided housing for black students and was a civil rights activist. Lemme Elementary in Iowa City is named for her. (A.)

Dottie Ray (1922–2016) was an editor-in-chief of the *Daily Iowan* newspaper. She began a radio program in 1959, interviewing a wide variety of guests. Her show ran until 2014, after compiling a remarkable list of over 32,000 guests on 14,444 shows. She was known for her ability to put her guests at ease with her cordial manner. (Amy Kanellis.)

June Braverman was a remarkable talent. She was a drummer with the Scottish Highlanders, later earned a PhD in educational administration, worked as a speech pathologist, and taught in two Iowa City high schools. While employed at the Iowa City Senior Center, she established a senior band that endures. She directed countless musical reviews and shows that benefited charitable organizations, playing piano by ear, able to transpose keys at the drop of a hat. She is seen here in Cuba playing for a show as part of her international aid work. (Tom Braverman family.)

William J. White and his son Robert J. are seen here around 1945. William served in World War I with the US Guards and also saw service in Texas in pursuit of Pancho Villa. A longtime Iowa City city assessor, William was also a master plumber. Robert served as a medic in World War II. Long-lived and very talkative Polly is seen on William's left shoulder. (Bob White.)

When a fire broke out involving Things, Things, and Things and other businesses in January 1970, firemen fought the blaze in bitterly cold conditions. In the aftermath, this amazing spectacle of ice was left on the sides of the buildings along College Street. (Oscar Beasley.)

In 1942, the University of Iowa established a war art workshop to prepare posters, instructional charts, graphs, and other visual aids for various agencies of the war effort. After the Japanese attack on Pearl Harbor in December 1941, it was feared that another attack could occur, even on the west coast of the United States. Accordingly, four practice blackouts were staged in San Francisco and a wide area around it within six days after the attack in Hawaii. Later, it was feared that the Atlantic Coast was vulnerable to attack by Germany. Subsequently, many other cities conducted blackouts. Even the middle section of the country saw rehearsals and when blackouts were staged in Iowa City in 1942, people wondered what could make Iowa City a possible target. The hosting of a naval preflight school program at the university was cited as a sufficient reason for preparedness. In this photograph, University of Iowa art instructor Alice Davis is examining posters prepared to advertise the coming blackout exercise in Iowa City on November 19, 1942. The posters declare, "No lights, stay off streets, park cars, don't telephone." Smoking outside was not permitted and no matches were to be lit outdoors or inside near windows. The event was heavily advertised and came off almost without a glitch. More blackouts followed, including at least one unannounced one. These exercises no doubt instilled anxiety and fear. Practice blackouts ceased in Iowa in late 1943 with more focus on "non-protective civilian defense activities, such as food production, salvage, and war financing." (FWK.)

The University of Iowa contracted with the US Navy to conduct preflight training for naval cadets. Shortly after this, other institutions were contracted for similar training. The last group of cadets to train at Iowa City began their work in May 1944. Future astronaut and senator John Glenn was one of the cadets trained in Iowa City. The fieldhouse and Quadrangle and Hillcrest men's dormitories were allocated for the Navy's use. Under the direction of aviation pioneer Paul Shaw and his team of some 23 flight instructors, 4 flight supervisors, 4 mechanics, 5 linemen, 5 office workers, and 41 aircraft, 2,500 pilots were trained in Iowa City. (FWK.)

In the early 1950s, when Procter & Gamble (P&G) decided to build a plant in Iowa City, the company received some pushback from city as well as university officials. The corporation flew 14 individuals, including university president Virgil Hancher and Iowa governor Leo Hoegh, to the headquarters in Cincinnati to show them how clean their plant was, not one that would spew polluting chemicals into the air. The Iowa City plant opened in 1956, leading the way to a resurgence of clean industrial growth in Iowa City. Owens Brush, later Oral B, opened a plant nearby, eventually capable of producing up to one million toothbrushes a day. Also, Victor Metals manufactured toothpaste tubes in a plant next to Procter & Gamble. When the P&G plant opened in Iowa City, one of its products was the newly patented fluoride-containing Crest toothpaste. The plant had the capacity to provide almost half of the toothpaste needs of the entire United States. Other companies, including Sheller Globe, H.P. Smith, Heinz, and others followed, all along Highway 6 East. (A.)

Irving Weber, 1900–1997, was a lifelong resident of Iowa City. He graduated from the University of Iowa where he was Iowa's first All-American swimmer. Weber spent his career in the wholesale dairy business and founded the Quality Checked Dairy Products Association. At age 72, he began a 25-year run of the publication of over 800 historical columns in the *Iowa City Press-Citizen* and reprinted them into eight volumes published by the Iowa City Noon Lions Club. All of the proceeds were donated to the Lions Club's sight and hearing conservation fund, amounting to over $60,000. Three years prior to his passing, a new Iowa City elementary school was named for him. Weber has been declared Iowa City's "unofficial official" historian. (A.)

This 1971 photograph shows a view to the southwest from the old University Hospital on Iowa Avenue. Only three structures of any height are seen, including Hotel Jefferson, which appears as the tallest. Behind it to the left is the court house and to the right, the Iowa State Bank building. Otherwise, the skyline is bereft of any tall structures. (Ray Bryant.)

This early 2023 photograph taken from the roof of Van Allen Hall shows a similar view as that in the 1971 image at the top of the page. A dramatic shift is seen, with many buildings now over 10 stories high, including one out of view to the right, effectively dwarfing Hotel Jefferson. Additional high-rises are being planned for downtown Iowa City. (A.)

DISCOVER THOUSANDS OF LOCAL HISTORY BOOKS FEATURING MILLIONS OF VINTAGE IMAGES

Arcadia Publishing, the leading local history publisher in the United States, is committed to making history accessible and meaningful through publishing books that celebrate and preserve the heritage of America's people and places.

Find more books like this at
www.arcadiapublishing.com

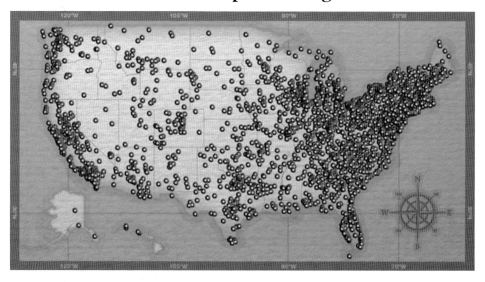

Search for your hometown history, your old stomping grounds, and even your favorite sports team.